KOKODA TRACK
101 DAYS

black dog

Peter Macinnis

First published in 2007 by
🐕 black dog books
15 Gertrude Street
Fitzroy Vic 3065
Australia
+61 3 9419 9406
+61 3 9419 1214 (fax)
dog@bdb.com.au

Peter Macinnis asserts the moral right to be identified as author of this Work.

Copyright text © Peter Macinnis

All rights reserved. Apart from any fair dealing for the purposes of study, research, criticism or review, as permitted under the Copyright Act, no part of this book may be reproduced by any process, stored in a retrieval system, or transmitted in any form, without permission of the copyright owner. All inquiries should be made to the publisher at the address above.

Designed by Blue Boat Design
Maps by Guy Holt Design
Printed and bound in Australia by Griffin Press

Cover Photographs credits:
Front Cover — 25-Pounder guns being pulled through dense jungle in the vicinity of Uberi on the Kokoda Track. AWM Image Number 026855.
Back Cover — Australian and American soldiers gaze at Salamaua. AWM Image Number 015394.

National Library of Australia
cataloguing-in-publication data:
Macinnis, P. (Peter).
    Kokoda track : 101 days.

    Bibliography.
    Includes index.
    ISBN 9781876372965.

    ISBN 1 876372 96 6.

    1. Australia. Army. Battalion, 39th - History - Juvenile literature. 2. World War, 1939-1945 - Campaigns - Papua New Guinea - Kokoda - Juvenile literature. I. Title. (Series : The drum).

940.541294

10 9 8 7 6 5 4 3   8/0123

Dedication

*I do not believe that I would be a good hero,
but if I ever had to try, the story of Kokoda offers many excellent models:
The war correspondents who reported back on the stupidities and evils of the Kokoda campaign,
and tried to get them fixed.
The generals who did the right thing by their troops,
and were sacked for doing so.
The men of the Australian and Japanese armies
who were forced by bad leaders to fight a foolish and pointless war. Neither side was well-served by its most senior commanders.
The airmen and pusher-outers who managed to keep the Australian troops supplied.
The irregulars, the old hands who knew the country
and made a difference.
The people of New Guinea who joined the Papuan Infantry Battalion, carried the loads and carried the wounded.
It wasn't their war, but they made it their war.
Peter Macinnis*

black dog books would like to dedicate this book to
*Frank Ballantyne (VX 148386) 1919–2005,
2/7th Australian Infantry Battalion*

Key People in These Events

Allied Commander-in-Chief
General Douglas MacArthur

Commander of Allied Forces
General Sir Thomas Blamey

Commander New Guinea Force
Major General Basil Morris (May 1941 to August 1942)
Lieutenant General Sydney Rowell (July to September 1942)
Lieutenant General Edmund Herring (from September 1942)

Commanders on the Kokoda Track
Major General Arthur 'Tubby' Allen (March to October 1942)
Major General George Vasey (September 1942 to end of campaign)
Brigadier Selwyn Porter (April 1942 to end of campaign)
Brigadier Arnold Potts (April to October 1942)
Brigadier Ken Eather (September 1942 to end of campaign)
Brigadier John Lloyd (October 1942 to end of campaign)

39th Battalion
Sergeant Major Jim Cowey
Lieutenant Simonson
Lieutenant Sam Templeton
Lieutenant William Merritt
Lieutenant Colonel William Taylor Owen

Japanese Imperial Army
Lieutenant General Hyakutake Harukichi
Major General Horii Tomitaro

War Correspondents
George Johnston
Osmar White
Chester Wilmot

List of Abbreviations

DSO — Distinguished Service Order

GHQ — General Headquarters

HMAS — His (or Her) Majesty's Australian Ship

LHQ — Land Headquarters

PIB — Papuan Infantry Battalion

NCO — Non-commissioned Officer (ranks below a lieutenant)

RAAF — Royal Australian Air Force

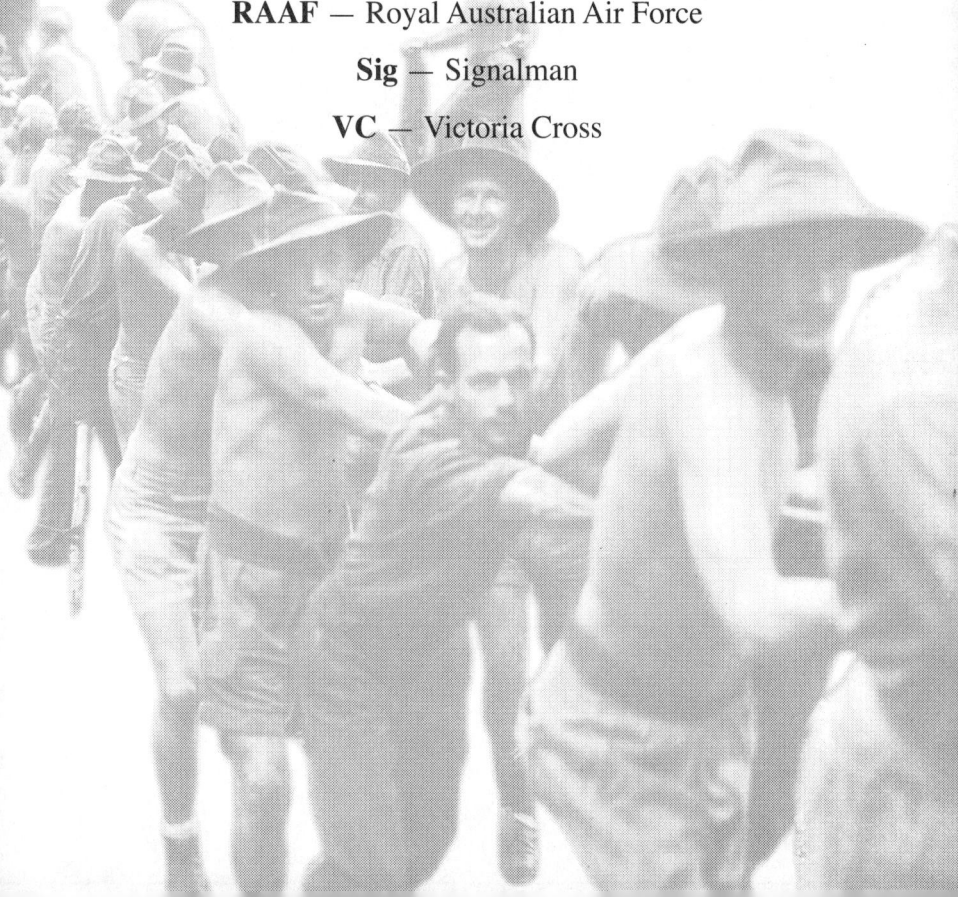

Sig — Signalman

VC — Victoria Cross

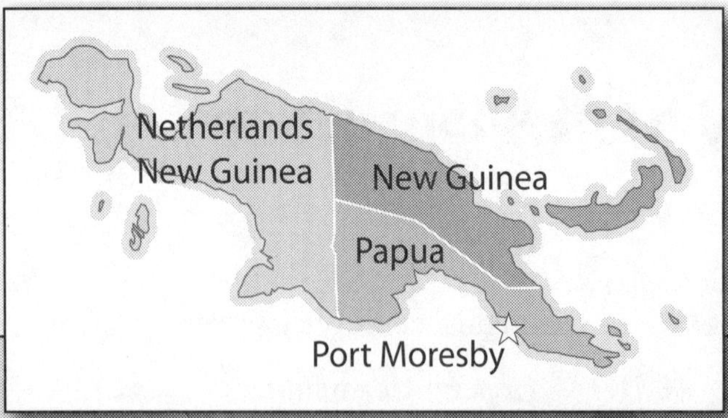
Netherlands New Guinea
New Guinea
Papua
Port Moresby

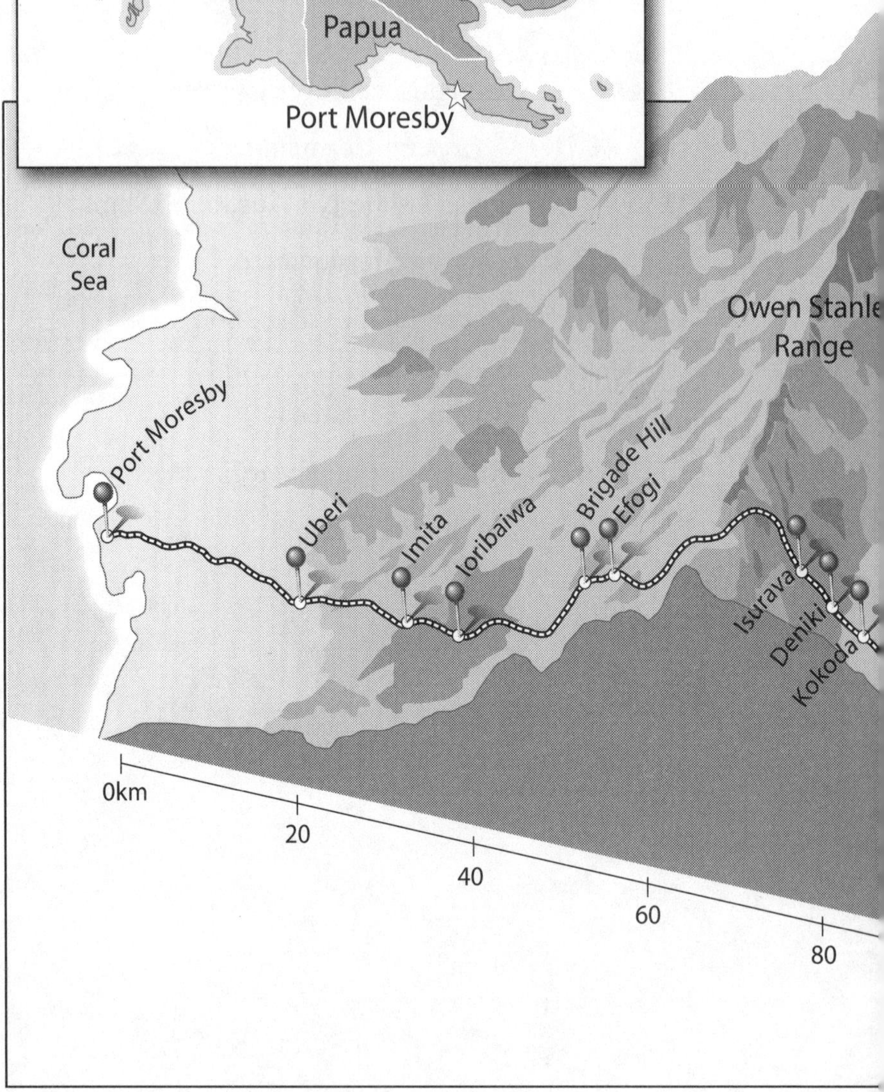
Coral Sea
Owen Stanle
Range
Port Moresby
Uberi
Imita
Ioribaiwa
Brigade Hill
Efogi
Isurava
Deniki
Kokoda
0km
20
40
60
80

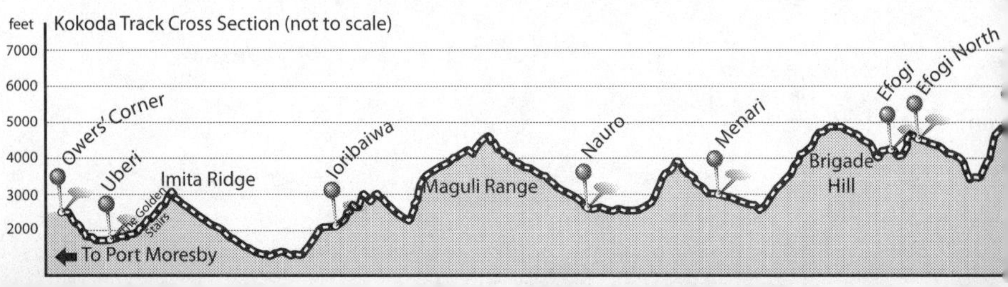
feet
Kokoda Track Cross Section (not to scale)
7000
6000
5000
4000
3000
2000
Owers' Corner
Uberi
The Golden Stairs
Imita Ridge
Ioribaiwa
Maguli Range
Nauro
Menari
Brigade Hill
Efogi
Efogi North
To Port Moresby

The Kokoda Track

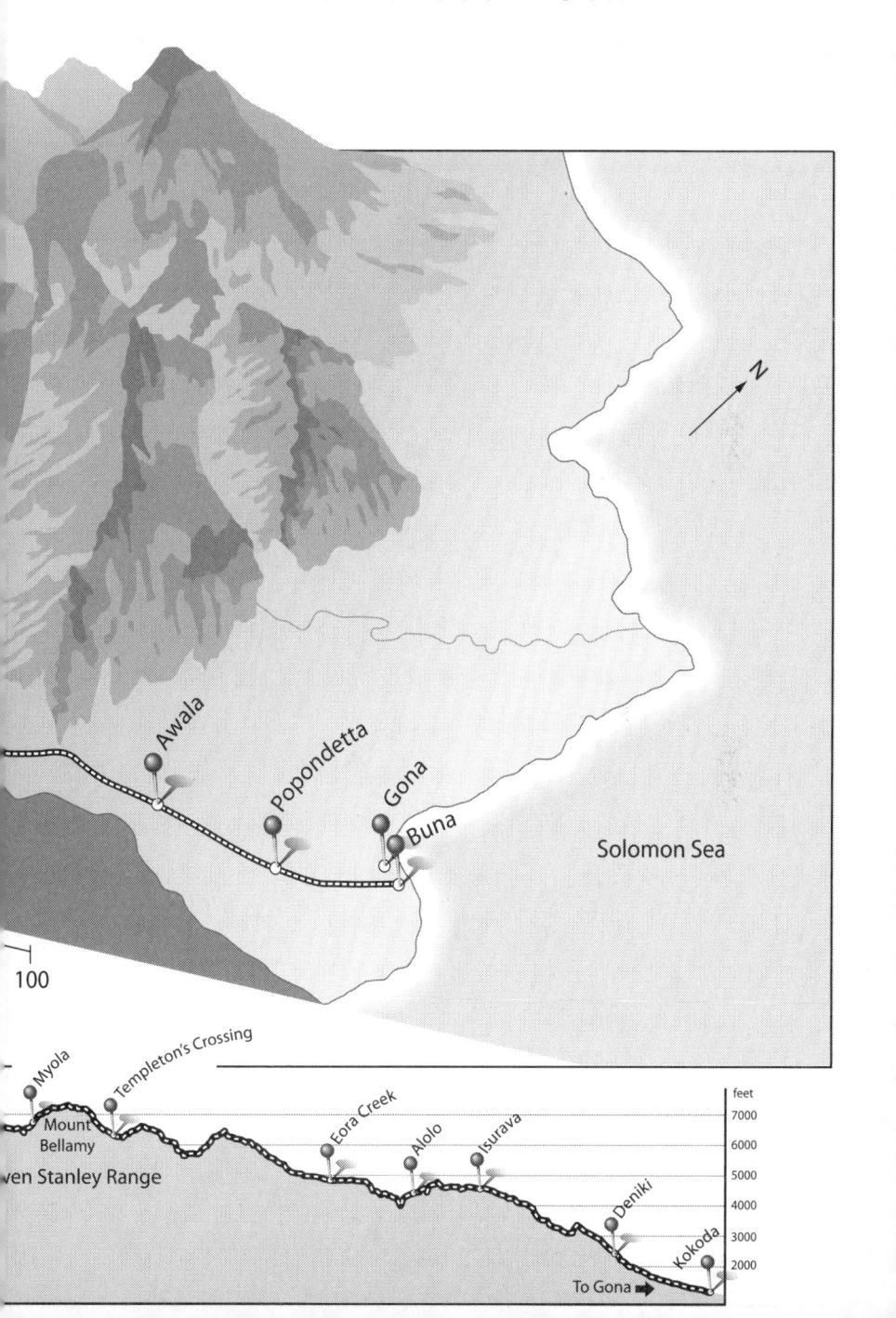

Contents

Introduction 3
Chapter 1: World War II Begins 13
Chapter 2: Keeping the Hope Alive 32
Chapter 3: Up the Track 48
Chapter 4: Kokoda and Deniki 66
Chapter 5: Fighting on the Track 89
Chapter 6: Tactics 103
Chapter 7: Australia's Thermopylae 112
Chapter 8: The Fight for Isurava 123
Chapter 9: General Horii's Plan Falters 135
Chapter 10: 101 Days — Australian Troops Enter Kokoda 156
Timeline 167
Glossary 169
Acknowledgments 171
References 172
Photos/Illustrations Credits 173
Index 175

World Map
1942

Imagine you are there...

'Charlie, how come you never talked about Kokoda?'

'It was a bastard of a place where a lot of good blokes got killed. We never wanted to talk about it when we came back. It took a long time for the story to be told.'

'But you won, didn't you? And against all odds?'

'Yeah, we won. And it was against a much larger force. But we did it with no help from the brass back home. They kept us short of ammo, supplied us with the wrong weapons, the wrong clobber, no blankets, no medical supplies, not enough food and no air support. There was no support. And when we came home, I guess we just wanted to forget about the whole sorry story.'

'Even though you won?'

'Yeah... We won ... But you know what? We were called a bunch of cowards by General Bloody Blamey. He told us we'd run like rabbits, then we got sent back to fight again. By then Blamey had sacked the commanders who'd fought with us — the ones who knew what we'd been through. We were left with new officers who believed Blamey's version. And they threw us in the thick of the fighting. They thought we needed punishing!'

'Okay, I can see why you might want to forget, but you were still heroes—'

'Not all of us, and not always. There were times when some of us ran and a few times when we panicked. But mostly we just pulled back a short way, regrouped, and fought again. And all the time there was a knot of fear in your guts that made you want to run. We all felt it.'

'Do you think you would run if you had to fight all over again?'

'Listen ... the thing about fighting a war ... it's all about confidence in yourself. Having confidence in your mates. Maybe, in a different time, in a different place ... maybe I would run.'

'But what Blamey said, that you ran like rabbits on the Track—'

'No, son, we never ran. We held the Japs up long enough on the Track for our reinforcements to come and help. That was all we needed to do, and we did it. I've always been proud of that.'

'Maybe if more people knew the story—'

'There's a good story there, for sure, but when you hear the politicians carry on, it's just sanitised malarkey. You have to tell the whole story — the good bits as well as the bad. You've got to leave the uncomfortable bits in, and don't suggest that war's glorious! Because it's not, son. It's not.'

Introduction

The story of the Kokoda Track is an extraordinary story of a small, largely untrained force, defeating one many times its size, despite the impediments placed in their path by their own commanders in Australia. This is the story of the first successful Allied offensive against the Japanese in the Pacific War in World War II.

For five brutal weeks in 1942, a mere 550 mainly young and inexperienced soldiers of the 39th Battalion, Australian militia soldiers, delayed an attacking force of 6000 experienced Japanese jungle troops who were crossing the Owen Stanley Range in Papua. The Japanese planned to secure Port Moresby as a base for future attacks in the region.

The Australian soldiers were outnumbered by a force, sometimes six to ten times their size. The tactic of the Australian military leaders on the track was to employ a fighting withdrawal. Fight, retreat, and fight again. Their stand at Isurava was a bloody battle that ensured the Japanese battle plan fell further and further behind schedule. The fighting withdrawal not only helped to slow down the advance of the Japanese over the Kokoda Track, it also ensured massive supply problems for the Japanese army and finally led to their defeat, as they withdrew back up the track without ever reaching Port Moresby.

The 39th were militia, not the volunteer soldiers of the Second Australian Imperial Force who had already established the reputation of the Australian soldier fighting in Europe and North Africa. The AIF contemptuously called the militia 'chockos', because they claimed the militia would melt in the sun like chocolate soldiers, at the first sign of pressure.

Though World War II began in 1939 the Japanese didn't enter the war until 7 December 1941. Then, over the next few months, they swept down through South-East Asia, taking country after country. After the Japanese were defeated at the Battle of the Coral Sea and the Battle of Midway they were blocked from attacking Port Moresby by sea. The Japanese were now looking for another route. In early July the Yokoyama Advance Force Unit, part of the Japanese Nankai Division, was ordered to investigate the possibility of invasion by landing on the north coast and crossing the Owen Stanley Range. They landed at Gona.

On 15 July news arrived that the Emperor, Hirohito, wished to occupy Port Moresby as soon as possible. Upon the strength of this, the mission turned into an invasion.

The remainder of the Japanese Nankai Division landed in Buna on 21 July 1942. Troops were sent into the jungle with just two week's rations.

The Japanese plan was to approach Port Morseby by trekking over the Owen Stanley Range along a series of tracks that became known as the Kokoda Track. The name was derived from the village of Kokoda, located on the northern side of the range.

The 39th defeated the Japanese by spoiling their plans for a quick victory. They did this by slowing down the Japanese advance until reinforced by the AIF — brought back from the Middle East to defend Australia — could arrive. The 39th fought, withdrew, established a new position, and fought again. They wore the Japanese down and stretched their supply lines. Even when the AIF arrived, the Australians were still outnumbered, and they continued the same plan of attack for another four weeks. The Japanese were eventually stopped at the summit near Ioribaiwa, 50 km north-east of Port Moresby. And later, when more troops arrived, the invaders were chased back over the mountains, and driven into the sea.

But the Japanese were not the only enemy with whom the Australian soldiers had to contend. There was the jungle, the weather, disease, and — perhaps most bitterly of all — the foolishness of their own senior command, headquartered in Australia. It was the troops on the ground — the officers and men — that won through.

The Japanese did not want America to use Australia as a base for an offensive campaign. If the Japanese had captured Port Moresby, they would have controlled access to Australia's airspace and sea lanes. Many Australians also saw the capture of Port Moresby

Soldier's Service Number

When someone joins the Australian military, they are given a service number which is used in defence records to administer and keep track of them — it's a bit like a tax file number today. In World War II, when someone joined the Australian army, they were given a service number which consisted of letters and numbers. The first letter stood for the state they were from. If they volunteered for the AIF they then had an 'X' followed by a number. Private Bruce Kingsbury's service number, for example, was VX19139. The 'V' was for Victoria, the 'X' for the AIF, and then his number. A soldier's service number, name, and religion were pressed onto their identity disc, which was made of metal and secured about the neck by a cotton thread, leather strip or metal chain.

as the first step to an invasion of Australia, though we now know that there were no such plans for invasion by the Japanese in 1942.

Before their New Guinea offensive, the Japanese had swept down through South-East Asia and invaded the Allied stronghold of Singapore. The battle for Singapore began on 7 February 1942 and the Japanese took the so-called 'impregnable fortress' on 15 February, resulting in the largest surrender of British-led military personnel in history.

The Allied counter-offensive successes on the Kokoda Track — pushing the Japanese in a retreat back up the track away from Port Moresby in late 1942 — and Milne Bay marked a shift in what had previously seemed the 'unstoppable force' of the Japanese army.

Today the Kokoda Track figures high in Australia's nationalist folklore, with everybody from footballers to rock stars tackling the track. But at the end of the World War II, the men who had fought this extraordinary action were largely forgotten and ignored. They returned home to their families, rarely speaking of what they'd undergone.

I was a war baby and heard a lot about World War II when I was growing up. At school, Kokoda did not figure largely on Anzac Day — or at any other time. We heard much more about Gallipoli and the 'Rats of Tobruk' — the Australian troops who fought in northern Africa against the Germans — than we did about Kokoda.

In 1961, when I was just 17, I left school and went to Port Moresby on work experience as a surveyor's assistant. I was the same age as the youngest men in the 39th Battalion. I still have a sense of how they may have felt being sent for the first time to a foreign land.

The war they had fought was finished before I had even begun to walk, but there was little change in the conditions at Port Moresby. I stepped off the plane into the heat and humidity of a country not far from the equator and felt confused

Kokoda Track or Kokoda Trail?
The word 'trail' probably originated with the Americans but it has been used in many history books and by the Australian Army as an official Battle Honour. The surviving war veterans I spoke to prefer the more Australian name 'Kokoda Track', and I have used that.

and overwhelmed. I had my family and friends to support me but the men of the 39th didn't even have tents to sleep in for the first few days after they arrived in Port Moresby.

During that stay I worked near the base of the Kokoda Track for a few weeks. The sun was intense and the humidity meant the air was like a heavy wet blanket. It was difficult to move in the heat of the day. The smells were rich and strong and clotted my nostrils. The sounds of the animals and birds were just as intense and the vegetation was strange.

We had four-wheel-drive trucks to carry us to and from our place of work. We had good supplies and all the equipment we needed. Best of all we could sing, laugh, cook our food and light our night without fear of being shot at. In 1942 the 39th soldiers had none of these luxuries. They either had the wrong equipment or not enough equipment, and what they were given, they had to carry.

During my visit, some of the 'old hands' were still around — men who had been there in wartime. I came across others who had yarned with the old hands. The men I worked with told me what it was like to have Japanese soldiers perched in trees, perfectly camouflaged, picking men off until somebody spotted and killed the sniper. This could take a while.

One of the surveyors warned me that the history books might have inaccurately reported that the Japanese were stopped up in the mountains. He showed me where he had found a pair of Japanese tree-climbing sandals, the kind snipers wore, close to the 'Seven-mile Strip'. This airstrip was located well past what the authorities called the limit of the Japanese advance. The sandals were just 11 kilometres from Port Moresby.

I worked for a time on that same disused airstrip, which was then about to become the University of Papua New Guinea. The long grass was littered with old ammunition that had never reached our troops. Each day we probably walked over unexploded Japanese bombs — dropped to destroy the planes that carried supplies to our troops up in the mountains — but I barely gave them a thought — not the ammunition, not the bombs, and certainly not the troops.

The idea of war only became real to me when a grass fire raced through the area one day and the old ammunition began exploding around us. My fellow workers and I ran.

We were lucky we could.

But the men of the 39th Battalion had to stay as bullets, mortar bombs and grenades snapped around them.

They dug in, they risked death, and many of them died.

New Guinea

New Guinea is a volcanic island where earthquakes are common. The island has a huge spine of rock, a chain of mountains named the Owen Stanley Range after a naval captain who mapped much of the coast in the 1840s. In places, the top of the range is 5 kilometres above sea level.

High mountains, combined with warm moist winds off the sea and monsoon weather, make for heavy rains, mist, fog, and sometimes even snow. The mountains are high enough for it to be bitterly cold at night, while the dry coastal plain near Port Moresby reaches mid-thirties temperatures daily.

This is a tropical island with volcanic soil, earthquakes and heavy rain, with a landscape of high mountains and steep valleys. Most of the rich soil is covered in dense jungle — a place where the treetops interlink to keep light and warmth away from the forest floor. There are wild pigs, tree kangaroos, wallabies and even several echidna species in New Guinea, but there is little else in the jungle to remind an Australian of home.

Imagine a letter written during the war...

Dear Beryl,

How's the weather? Not too hot for you, I hope.

We've had a letter from Ernie. We miss him terribly, but Reg seems to be suffering the most. Not that he'd tell you, of course. He spends a lot of time out in the shed with the wireless, hammering and banging about and not much to show for it.

There wasn't much news about the fighting, but Ernie says your Harry is fit and well. They were on leave at the same place 'somewhere in the Middle East'. Have you heard from Harry?

The town's Red Cross Auxiliary is livelier than it was when you lived here. Mrs Nose-in-the-air has been swanning around, boasting how her son, Barry, is 'doing his bit', when he is only in the militia.

People are fed up with Mrs N.

Most members have sons in the AIF. Poor Miss Davies, who lost her fiancé at Lone Pine, has never married. I wonder how many of our daughters will face the same fate — unmarried like Miss Davies because the best and brightest boys have gone off and been killed. And Mrs N carries on about how we are equal in our sacrifice!

Word around town is that the real soldiers are calling

the militia koalas, because they are not to be shot at or exported from Australia! Somebody must have thought this was funny because they stuck a drawing of a koala on the noticeboard in the Auxiliary rooms. It has a rifle with a toilet brush for a bayonet. It looks just like Mrs N's Barry, but she hasn't said a word. I reckon Gladys did it. She has three sons in the AIF, and you know how she feels about Mrs N!

Mrs N's darling Barry has been shipped over to New Guinea. Reg says he has seen the paperwork in his paper-shuffling job at Vic Barracks and the militia are just building roads. It's not like Barry is at the front line — the Japs are never going to worry about New Guinea.

I don't understand it, Beryl. My Reg and your Alf are too long in the tooth to fight, so they're doing their bit in other ways, but these young boys in the militia are just allowed to sit on the sidelines, out of harm's way. I say hand their work to the older blokes, winkle the militia out of their cushy jobs and send them off to the real fight. Our boys in the AIF need a break.

Love all round.

Chapter 1
World War II Begins

The official start of World War II was 1939. Australia was then very much part of the British Empire — the large part of the world that was then coloured red on Australian school maps. Many people boasted that the sun never set on the British Empire. What they meant was that as the earth revolved through its 24-hour cycle, there was always a part of the British Empire which was in sunlight.

Because Australia was part of the British Empire, it was seen as an extension of Britain. Many Australians at the time referred to Britain as 'home'. When Britain declared war on Germany on 3 September 1939, the Australian Prime Minister, Robert Menzies, announced on the radio: 'Fellow Australians, it is my melancholy duty to inform you officially that, in consequence of a persistence by Germany in her invasion of Poland, Great Britain has declared war upon her and that as a result, Australia is also at war.'

In one sense, World War II was fought between the 'haves' and the 'have-nots'. The Germans had no colonies to source raw materials from for their growing factories and few colonies to buy what they produced. The Japanese only had access to China and

Korea, while Italy had access to colonial territories in the Middle East in what is now known as Libya. In contrast, the British Empire was huge, the French had large colonies in Indo-China and Africa, and the Dutch held Indonesia as a colony. The United States of America (USA) had a few colonies, including the Philippine Islands. (The USA were in the process of making the Philippines an independent country when Japan invaded it.) But the USA could source raw materials from Central and South America and trade with their markets in almost the same way that the British and the French traded with their empires.

In 1931, before the declaration of war, the Japanese army had invaded parts of China. But while many Australians worried about the Japanese, they felt protected by the British Navy, stationed at Singapore.

In 1941, Australians assumed that if Australia was under threat of attack, Britain would come to the rescue. Unfortunately, this proved not to be the case.

Australians in Europe

Most RAAF (Royal Australian Air Force) personnel served in RAF squadrons in Britain during World War II. At the beginning of the war, only two Australian RAAF squadrons were overseas.

The AIF soldiers were all volunteers. In Australia, the army began recruiting and training soldiers, ready to send them across the globe to fight for Britain and the Empire, just as it had done in World War I. The original World War I troops were called the Australian Imperial Force, or AIF, so in this new war, the Australians were known as the Second AIF, and they were headed for Europe and the Mediterranean. They fought in Greece, Crete, North Africa, and in Syria, in an area that is now southern Lebanon.

By January 1942, the core of Australia's army, navy and air force had been deployed to Europe and North Africa. There were over 120,000 Australian troops overseas at this time. When Rabaul on the island of New Britain, just north of New Guinea and part of the Australian administrative territory, was invaded by the Japanese in January, Australia was virtually unprotected!

Japan enters the war

In 1939, at the start of the war, the Japanese controlled some Pacific islands in what is now known as Micronesia. Japan fought on the side of the Allies in World War I, and seized Chuuk (Truk), Pohnpei (Ponape) and other islands from the Germans in 1914. Later, the islands became League of Nations territories under Japan's control and they became useful bases for the Japanese when World War II began.

Even before the war began in Europe, Australians were apprehensive about Japan and its expansionist policies. The Japanese had brutally invaded China in 1931. Then, in July 1941, the Vichy French government let the Japanese army move into Indo-China. The US

Papua and New Guinea

In 1942 there were two halves to Papua New Guinea. Australia administered the southern side of Papua, while the northern side, New Guinea, had been taken from Germany in World War I. New Guinea was held as a trust territory through the League of Nations — the forerunner of the United Nations, which was formed after World War I. Australia governed and administered Papua and New Guinea differently. There were different rules and different conditions for each territory.

President, Franklin D. Roosevelt, countered this threat by putting Japan under an oil embargo. This meant the Japanese navy would run out of oil by mid-1942. Faced with the possibility of running out of fuel, the Japanese declared war on the US.

On 7 December 1941, the Japanese navy launched a surprise attack on the US base at Pearl Harbor in Hawaii. Their plan was to cripple the US navy and to destroy as many aircraft as possible, ensuring the US was no match for the Japanese aircraft carriers — carriers that Japan thought would ensure their victory.

At almost the same time, Japanese forces landed in Malaya and began sweeping down toward the great fortress of Singapore. In a little over two months, on 15 February 1942, Singapore surrendered to Japan.

During the next three and a half years, 22,000 Australians were captured on Singapore and other islands and became prisoners of war. Most of these were from the

8th Division and were captured in Singapore. Of the 22,000 taken captive, 8000 prisoners died.

The Japanese army was also snapping up the islands of Indonesia. In late January they captured Rabaul on the island of New Britain, which gave them a port and airfields in easy reach of New Guinea. The day after Pearl Harbor, Japanese troops landed on Guam and on Midway and Wake Islands. They also attacked Hong Kong.

Allied Powers
In the early days of the war against Japan, they were referred to as ABDA, meaning American, British, Dutch and Australian. For most of World War II, the only allies in Australia's region were the US and Australia. A number of other countries fought on the side of the Allies in Europe, including Russia and Canada.

Australia's allies

A notable aspect of World War II is the way Australia switched its allegiance from Britain as its main ally to the United States. Many assume that this switch came after Britain tried to stop the Australian government from bringing its troops home from Europe and North Africa to defend Australia from the Japanese threat, which would have left Australia undefended. In reality, the switch came long before that.

In 1941 the Australian Prime Minister, Robert Menzies, was

A Turning Point in Australian History
In late December 1941, Curtin famously wrote in a newspaper: 'Without any inhibitions of any kind, I make it quite clear that Australia looks to America, free of any pangs as to our traditional links or kinship with the United Kingdom.'

replaced after he lost the support of his own party. John Curtin became prime minister in a Labor government in October 1941, as the Japanese war became more certain. The Prime Minister of the United Kingdom at the time was Winston Churchill. Sir Winston Churchill was an English statesman and author and was to become one of the most important leaders in world history.

Two of the most powerful British battleships, *Prince of Wales* and *Repulse*, had been sunk by Japanese aircraft on 10 December off the coast of Malaya. Curtin quickly saw that Britain would never be able to defend Australia in the same way Australia had fought for Britain. The only nation now capable of helping Australia was the USA. It was in the interests of America to help Australia — if only to use Australia as a base — and Curtin was willing to do whatever it took to ensure that Australia was saved from invasion.

Curtin's timely article was a turning point in Australian history, in which Australia defined itself as an independent nation, not just an outpost of the British Empire, as well as turning away from the traditional links to England and looking to the United States. It was also a clever appeal to the United States for help.

If John Curtin had any lingering hopes that Britain might help, the disastrous Battle of the Java Sea and the later Battle of the Sunda Strait saw 13 ships — four Dutch, four British, four from the US and HMAS *Perth* — all sunk. It was the end of British naval power in Asian waters and the end of Dutch power, leaving only Australian and American ships to fight off the invaders.

At the start of the war, Australia sent its fittest and best-trained soldiers to fight the enemy overseas, leaving just the poorly-trained and poorly-equipped militia to defend Australia.

As the war crept closer to Australian shores, Curtin found that his British allies did not have the same enthusiasm for saving Australia as Australia had for saving Britain. Churchill preferred to save India, because it was a valuable colony. He wanted the AIF troops returning from Syria to be diverted to Burma to fight the Japanese instead of returning to Australia. He even persuaded US President Roosevelt to pressure Curtin to agree.

But Curtin would not relent and his party backed him all the way. Curtin insisted that the AIF should return immediately to Australia. But Churchill would

War Comes to Australia, 19 February 1942
'So suddenly did the Japanese air fleet appear that Darwin was completely surprised... from the south-east 17 silver Japanese bombers appeared flying in formation at nearly 20,000 feet. The whistle of the falling bombs reached a shrill crescendo culminating in a terrific blast... For the first time bombs had fallen on Australian soil. For the first time Australians had been killed in their own homes by an act of war. War had at last really come to Australia.'
— Soldier VX115, *Soldiering On* published by Australian War Memorial, Canberra, ACT 1942.

not accept that answer. He again asked Curtin to make the troops available for the Burma campaign and, without waiting for an answer, ordered the ships to be diverted. It was now late February 1942 and again Curtin demanded the return of Australian troops to Australia, where they were needed. Timor had been attacked and the Japanese were starting to cut Australia off from the rest of the world. With bad grace, Churchill agreed to allow Australia's troops to return to their homeland. Six weeks later, the Japanese army controlled Burma, but Australia had a reserve of trained and experienced troops. As we will see, they were not the troops who saved Australia, but they finished the job the militia began.

Australia at war

When a country is threatened by war, its leaders have to fight several battles. Within their own party, there will be people trying to replace them, as Menzies found. Then there will be other political parties trying to bring down the government, because they think they can manage the war better. Then leaders have to fight with their country's allies for a share of resources and credit. Only then can they think about fighting the enemy.

Military leaders have their own pressures. They must deal with nervous politicians and senior officers within their ranks who are forever seeking promotion opportunities.

The voters are easily alarmed. When citizens think they may be on the losing side, the war effort suffers. Little things like rationing can get people worried, but when they come under fire, panic sets in. This could explain Japan's strategy of bombing Darwin in early 1942 and why a Japanese submarine shelled Sydney and Newcastle while Japanese midget submarines attacked Sydney Harbour.

MacArthur and Blamey in charge

By March 1942, US forces were engaged in a losing battle in the Philippines. The US president, Franklin D. Roosevelt, with Prime Minister Curtin's approval, ordered General Douglas MacArthur to leave the Philippines and relocate to Australia to take charge of the Allied forces in the Pacific. Once MacArthur was in charge, US troops and supplies began to arrive in Australia.

It was appropriate that with the US carrying most of the cost of the Pacific military venture

I Shall Return

'The President of the United States ordered me to break through the Japanese lines and proceed from Corregidor to Australia for the purpose ... of organizing the American offensive against Japan, a primary objective of which is the relief of the Philippines. I came through and I shall return.' General Douglas MacArthur, remarks to reporters in Australia after he had been ordered by President Roosevelt to leave the fortress on the island of Corregidor in the Philippines before it fell to the Japanese — 30 March 1942.

an American would head the operation. Australia's contribution was to appoint General Thomas Blamey as Commander-in-Chief of the Australian Military Forces on 11 March 1942. When General Blamey arrived in Melbourne on 26 March 1942, he was also appointed Commander-in-Chief of Allied Land Forces. He would be working under the new Commander-in-Chief of the South West Pacific Area, General Douglas MacArthur.

While there was no language barrier between the people of United States and of Australia, there were significant cultural differences. MacArthur did not understand the Australian character and the Australians didn't understand MacArthur and his American commanders. By surrounding himself with his own countrymen, MacArthur failed to see the gap between his command and Australian concerns. Australians wanted to push the war away from their door, while MacArthur's first concern was to win the Philippines back. The Prime Minister's War Conference, consisting of the Prime Minister and General MacArthur, was established after MacArthur and Blamey had been appointed to their new commands. MacArthur became the government's main advisor and Blamey took offence at his exclusion. It was the first of many slights that Thomas Blamey was to endure. Still, MacArthur was in Australia, and the Australian people felt more comfortable knowing he was there. While MacArthur was in Australia, the US provided whatever the general demanded. Code experts, aircraft, anything could be obtained through the general. Nobody cared if he wanted all the glory, so long as it did not interfere with fighting the war, but soon enough, MacArthur's craving for glory interfered terribly with the Papua New Guinea campaign.

Dugout Doug
General MacArthur was given the nickname 'Dugout Doug' in the Philippines campaign, when he spent long periods in the bomb shelters of Allied Headquarters at Corregidor — an island at the entrance of the Philippines' Manila Bay.

Thomas Blamey

Thomas Blamey was ambitious. As a young man he had visions of life as a clergyman but instead became

General Thomas Blamey, General Douglas MacArthur and the Prime Minister of Australia, John Curtin.

a schoolteacher in Western Australia. He then moved onto a military career, joined a school cadet unit, and chased promotion. In 1910, he joined the Citizen Military Forces with the rank of captain. In 1912, Blamey was sent to Staff College in India, to learn all about military planning.

By 1914, Blamey had visited Germany, Belgium and the Turkish coastline near Gallipoli. Then he was promoted to the position of major and relocated to England. He was sent to Egypt in November 1914, and landed at Gallipoli at 7.30 a.m. on 25 April 1915 where he remained until he was evacuated in August — with a bad case of piles. His only close-hand experience of the enemy came when he went out on patrol with a bombardier and a sergeant, in an effort to find the location of some hidden Turkish guns.

Blamey was a skilled staff officer, attending to paper work and administration. He served on the Western Front under commanders such as General, later Sir, John Monash.

At the outbreak of World War II, Blamey was appointed to command the Second Australian Imperial Force in the Middle East. Blamey's subordinate senior army officers were divided between 'Blamey men' and those who weren't. He had many supporters among senior officers, however he was not popular with the ordinary soldier. He hated the media and would not allow any negative information to reach the public.

I interviewed one of the last survivors of Blamey's staff while I was researching this book, and asked him what he thought of Blamey. He pointed one thumb down.

'Brilliant but a complete bastard,' he said.

From what he and others have reported, if Thomas Blamey had been in charge of loading the ships that took the 39th and 53rd battalions to Port Moresby, their camping gear would have been at the top, not at the bottom of a hold. Blamey was meticulous, and he demanded the same attention to detail from those under him — but he lacked humanity and was neither a tactician nor a strategist.

The AIF and the militia

In World War II, Australia's army was divided in two. First there was the AIF who were volunteers and a force that could be sent anywhere. The other soldiers were the militia who were either conscripts or were too young to join the AIF. To be a volunteer in the AIF, a soldier had to be over 21 years of age or have a parent's permission. The militia were only able to serve in Australian territory whereas the AIF could serve anywhere in the world.

The AIF soldiers considered the militia below their standards. The militia were regarded as cowards for not volunteering at the outbreak of the war. Because the militia were only required to serve in Australia, they also known as 'koalas: not to be shot at or exported'.

The militia had the most unpleasant jobs, the worst equipment, the oldest officers, and, for the most part, received very little training. These were not the men you would send into battle to save Australia. In the end somebody did send the militia into battle. In 1942, 60,000 of Australia's best soldiers were overseas.

Prime Minister Curtin understood that these soldiers needed to return to Australia and that the divided army should become one fighting unit. Getting the AIF to return, though, took several months. There was little choice but to send the militia to New Guinea. It was time for these soldiers to show everyone that they were up to the job. And they did.

Mills Grenade

The grenades used by the Australians were bigger and more deadly than the Japanese grenades. Japanese survivors commented later on the accuracy with which they were thrown over great distances — one of the lesser advantages of being a cricketing nation, perhaps.

The Mills grenade had a lethal quality when compared with the lighter Japanese grenade. It was fitted with a four-second fuse and was a classic 'pineapple' design of cast iron with grooves.

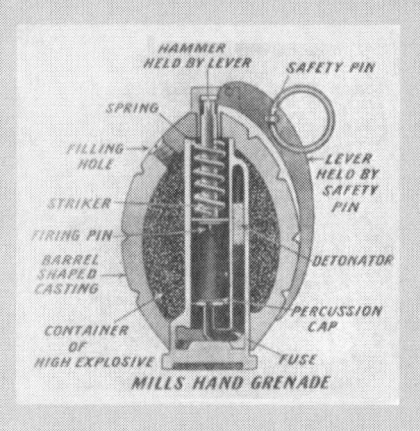

Army Terms

You can't talk about the army without understanding a few basic terms. The biggest unit I will mention is a division, made up of three brigades, and commanded by a major-general. A brigade is made up of three battalions, commanded by a brigadier or, as the Americans say, a one-star general.

Usually a battalion is commanded by a lieutenant colonel and made up of five parts: A, B, C, D Companies and HQ Company, each of around 100 to 110 men. Each of the companies would be commanded by a captain or a major, and the company would be divided into three platoons of 38 men, each commanded by a lieutenant, and each platoon would have three sections of 10 under a corporal or sergeant.

The army also needs extra people to manage food, cooking, medical matters, signals and stores. These soldiers were often older and less fit, and were called either 'the old and the bold' or 'the toothless and the ruthless', but the army ran because of them. In some cases there was a separate E company for machine-guns. The militia kept their E companies until 1943 — they were part of the battalion. The 39th Battalion had a machine-gun company.

Keeping it simple, the ranks in the army from bottom up are private, then the NCO (non-commissioned officer), lance corporal, corporal, warrant officer and sergeant. Then there are the commissioned officers: lieutenant, captain, major, lieutenant colonel, colonel, brigadier, and major-general.

Basic Army Structure

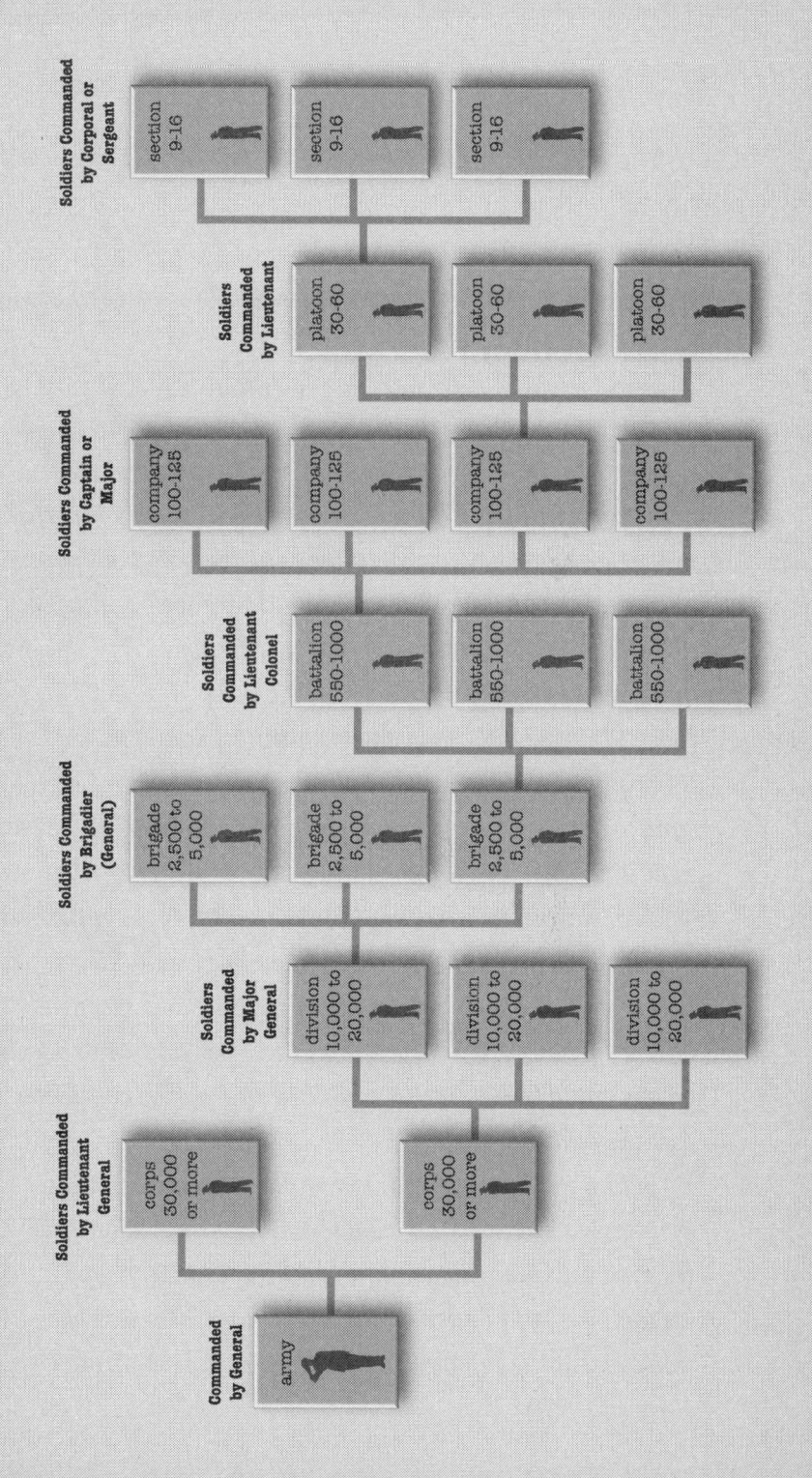

Commanded by General
- army

Soldiers Commanded by Lieutenant General
- corps 30,000 or more
- corps 30,000 or more

Soldiers Commanded by Major General
- division 10,000 to 20,000
- division 10,000 to 20,000
- division 10,000 to 20,000

Soldiers Commanded by Brigadier (General)
- brigade 2,500 to 5,000
- brigade 2,500 to 5,000
- brigade 2,500 to 5,000

Soldiers Commanded by Lieutenant Colonel
- battalion 550-1000
- battalion 550-1000
- battalion 550-1000

Soldiers Commanded by Captain or Major
- company 100-125
- company 100-125
- company 100-125
- company 100-125

Soldiers Commanded by Lieutenant
- platoon 30-60
- platoon 30-60
- platoon 30-60

Soldiers Commanded by Corporal or Sergeant
- section 9-16
- section 9-16
- section 9-16

Imagine a report from a war correspondent...

The press at home reported what they were told and GHQ (General Headquarters) played down what was happening in New Guinea. Everything that was reported was censored. They probably thought there was no point alarming the citizens. I wonder if Australians really wanted to know what was going on, anyway.

I was a war correspondent in the thick of it, but that didn't mean I reported everything I saw. The correspondent's job was to help the war effort, and sometimes that meant ignoring things. Besides, the censors would never let us say too much.

We kept our eyes open and made notes. If we got access to sensible commanders, we let them know what was happening. We were eating army rations, and that was how we paid our way, by being extra eyes and ears. See, the troops could talk to us, so could the orderlies, the padres and the officers.

Before the Japs arrived, we could see New Guinea was a mess. No strength, no leadership, nothing! The militia troops knew more about tropical diseases than about weapons — and I suspect they had more diseases than weapons! If the Japanese had attacked Moresby from the sea, the way they planned, our organised defences would not have lasted more than 48 hours.

But we didn't report that.

Printing such information would only frighten the Australian public and be unfair to the boys fighting there.

Our soldiers had spirit. I'll never forget one boy who thumbed a ride from the airfield to the town. His face was so badly bitten by insects that he had been unable to shave for a week. His knees and lower legs were encased in scabs that oozed serum and pus. Someone in the car accused him of scratching his scabs.

His miserable eyes almost gave the answer. 'I don't when I'm awake,' he muttered. 'But a man can't help himself when he's asleep.'

Still, these lads had a sense of humour. A grader crew was caught out in the open in one air raid, so they took shelter under the machine. The problem was that they were on a hill, and the driver had forgotten to put the machine in gear. As the bombs began to fall, the grader began to roll down the hill.

Naturally enough, the shelterers started to crawl along with the grader, but as the machine gathered speed, they were left behind, still crawling, noses down, as the grader outpaced them. When they realised, they laughed their heads off.

How can you report the truth about people with a spirit like that, and deny them a tiny bit of hope?

So to an extent, I never did.

Chapter 2
Keeping the Hope Alive

The first battalion of militia sent to Papua was the 49th Battalion. The men in the 49th were Queenslanders who had volunteered to work in tropical areas. They reached Port Moresby in March 1941 where they were put to work building roads, unloading ships, erecting buildings and readying Port Moresby in case war arrived.

There were about 6000 Europeans in PNG at the time, with 4500 Europeans on the New Guinea side and 1500 on the Papuan side.

Almost a year later, two more militia battalions — the 39th and 53rd — arrived in Port Moresby. They disembarked in January at the start of the wet season, just as I did, many years later. The temperature would have hit 38°C each day, and the humidity would have been close to 100 per cent before the rain started just after lunch. Then the clouds would roll away, the sun would shine again, and the sweat would begin to roll off the body.

Even at night when the temperature dropped, the humidity was so high that soldiers were still bathed in sweat. If they did not drink water and take salt tablets, they risked getting ill. If they did drink the water, they risked getting ill from the bugs that infested it. Even when soldiers ate well (which was not often) they lost weight. During my stay in Port Moresby I lost 20 per cent of my body weight, in ten days, from 44 kg down to 36 kg. So to this paradise came the 39th and 53rd. And though they arrived together, the two battalions had almost nothing else in common.

The NSW militia battalion, the 53rd, had a flawed beginning. To make up the numbers, 100 raw recruits were added to a random gathering taken from many other battalions, so the 53rd started out as a bunch of strangers. Some were rounded up from the streets of Sydney for immediate departure to Port Moresby. Many did not get a chance to farewell their families which caused immediate hostility and unrest among the battalion. Men who are going to work as a military unit are like a family. You know your immediate family very well, and you know your extended family well enough. It is the familiarisation that ensures battalions work well together.

The 39th Battalion came from Victoria, and they were together for several months before they were sent to New Guinea as a unit. They had more training than the 53rd and had better officers — men with more experience. If you are going to rely on people in a life-or-death situation, you need to know you can count on them and the 39th had more of that confidence in each other. There has been talk that the 39th were a 'young battalion', but the average age was approximately 24 years. In Isurava and afterwards, they were lucky to fall under the command of Lieutenant Colonel Ralph Honner. They were the first battalion to resist the Japanese on Australian territory and wore this honour proudly.

In January 1942, the 39th, 49th and 53rd battalions joined to become the one full-strength brigade in Papua at this time. They were the 30th Brigade.

Conditions for the militia

The new militia arrivals were set to work in Port Moresby to join the 49th in the task of unloading ships and building landing fields for aircraft. They wore only shirts, shorts and boots, and were driven almost mad by mosquitoes, flies and other pests. To begin with they had no camping equipment at all, because it was the first thing loaded onto their ships and thus the last to be unloaded. Until the ships were fully unloaded, life was very unpleasant.

With the general lack of hygiene among the poorly trained soldiers, most of them suffered the 'trots' (bacillary dysentery) which required frequent visits to the latrines. The pit-latrine toilets were so bad that men with delicate stomachs wore their gas masks when they paid a visit.

Within a month, dengue fever, malaria, dysentery and tropical ulcers had made 25 per cent of the soldiers unfit to work. They had lost about 20 pounds (9 kilograms) each, and many of their bites had become infected. As they walked through the grass, tiny little

Private P. Shimmin starts on his daily ration of bully beef straight out of the tin.

Good Enough to Eat
A section of 11 men had to share 5 pounds of rice and a one-pound tin of beef each day. In a good week, the food was baked beans, tinned corned beef, rice, soggy bread, and rancid and oily tinned butter. Occasionally there was jam — if the ants didn't get to it first!

mites called mockas invaded their socks until soldiers were nearly driven mad by the irritation of the hard lumps that circled their ankles. They called it 'scrub itch', and as they walked, they would stop to scratch first one ankle, then the other. It wasn't long before the scratched bites became infected.

It's possible to get tropical ulcers as far south as Sydney, but they were much worse in New Guinea. Any bite that was scratched became damp and attracted flies. Before the soldiers knew it, the bite became a weeping sore that got deeper and deeper. Soon it became a tropical

Malaria
There was no vaccine for malaria in 1942, just as there isn't today. At the end of the New Guinea campaign, there were over 9000 Australian soldiers suffering from malaria compared with 2037 killed and 3533 wounded.

ulcer, which needed to be covered in antiseptic cream and bandaged. The dressing needed changing every day for weeks until it healed. Smaller scratches were covered in red Mercurochrome until the bare legs beneath the regulation shorts were just a mass of red stains.

There was little time for the militia to get away from their work of unloading ships and building airfields, so there was little time for soldiering or training. There was no jungle training. The weapons they were supplied with were left over from World War I. Few could fire their rifles correctly.

Bombing begins

The first Japanese air raid on Port Moresby occurred on 3 February 1942. The Japanese began flying over the Owen Stanley Range from Rabaul on bombing raids. The bombers stayed at around 7000 metres, too far up for any guns to reach them, but also too high for accurate bombing. It was enough, though, to make some of the New Guinean workers leave town. Some even crossed the highest mountains and went to Kokoda on the other side of the range.

Then, in early March 1942, the Japanese landed on the northern side of New Guinea, around Lae and Salamaua.

Within a week, Allied pilots flying over Lae confirmed that an invasion force was being assembled, and Port Moresby seemed the likely target. US bombers from two aircraft carriers, *Lexington* and *Yorktown*, attacked and largely destroyed the force, postponing any invasion.

But the military commanders grew apprehensive.

Brigadier Porter takes command

In the middle of April 1942, Brigadier Porter took command of the Australian troops in Port Moresby and found aged and unfit men in the 30th Brigade with little battle experience. They were armed with weapons that were 30 to 40 years old. Equipment of every kind was in short supply because any new weapons went to the AIF troops, who were regarded as the front line.

Porter weeded out the older and unfit officers, replacing 36 of them with AIF officers. The 53rd Battalion received two captains and six lieutenants, the 49th Battalion got a major, five captains and six lieutenants. The 39th Battalion received almost half of the new officers, including a new commander, a major, six captains and eight lieutenants. Not only did the 39th get the largest share of the new officers but, more importantly, three of the captains replaced earlier company commanders.

By the time Porter was finished, there was only one officer in the 39th Battalion who had served in World War I. That officer, Lieutenant Sam Templeton, was a former submariner who had also fought in the Spanish Civil War. According to his platoon commanders, Templeton was 'at least 50', but he and Lieutenant William Merritt were selected from the existing 39th officers, promoted to the rank of captain, and given a company each to command. The 53rd Battalion companies kept their old commanders.

Training begins for the militia

The new officers were dismayed by their new troops. Still, they could see how training and discipline could bring about a positive change in the soldiers. Training, such as it was, was based on the idea that the Japanese would invade from the sea. Most of the old hands, the men who knew the country, had their 'whizz-through' bags for the Daru Derby at the ready.

The old hands planned to head off through trackless jungle, bush and delta swamps for 400 miles to Daru — an island off the coast — with little more than trade tobacco and emergency gear. These men had no idea of dying an honourable and useless death, when they could survive to fight another day. The militia would be expected to stay behind in trenches, shooting with rifles at the invaders who stormed ashore, but their job was only to delay the inevitable. They were speed bumps, not a barrier.

All the same, the militia were now being taught to handle their weapons, to defend and to fight. The 39th Battalion had more of the new AIF officers, so they progressed faster than the other battalions.

In late May, just five weeks before the 39th Battalion went into action, the 30th Brigade was graded 'F'. This meant their training was incomplete. They were not a force ready for battle.

The militia had trained on the open, dry, flat coastal plain in Port Moresby where impressive rainforest patches lay between areas of open woodland of grass and gum trees. The soldiers trained to fight only in the open areas. It was not the sort of training troops needed to fight in the high country of the Owen Stanley Range, but everybody believed the Japanese would attack Port Moresby from the sea.

The Battle of the Coral Sea

There were reasons to assume the Japanese forces would come by sea. Ten days after Rabaul, on the island of New Britain, fell in February 1942, General Syd Rowell sent a warning to Major General Basil Morris, the General Officer Commanding, New Guinea Force at that time, that a land attack was possible.

After the war, Morris was criticised for doing nothing, but he did send out a patrol made up of

General Sydney Fairbairn Rowell

Educated at Adelaide High School, General Sydney Rowell was one of the first cadets at the Royal Military College, Duntroon. Like Thomas Blamey, Rowell only gained a small amount of combat experience in World War I. Unlike Blamey, Syd Rowell had the respect of his soldiers.

In October 1939 Rowell was appointed Chief of Staff of the 6th Division, AIF. In 1940, Blamey appointed Rowell as Brigadier, General Staff, and in March 1942 Rowell became a temporary Lieutenant General in charge of the defence of southern Queensland. He was moved to Port Moresby in July 1942 as Commander of the New Guinea Force.

He asked war correspondent Chester Wilmot to write a full report on the state of soldiers and conditions in New Guinea, explaining what the troops needed, and then he sent it to Land Headquarters (LHQ), which was Blamey's command, and suggested that copies be issued to all troops coming in.

Rowell was the first to predict that the Japanese might attempt an attack across New Guinea, as far back as February 1942. General Rowell preferred not to send his troops into glorious defeats when waiting would wear the Japanese down and give his troops a useful advantage. Rowell sent strong messages back to Douglas MacArthur, Thomas Blamey, and their staff to make it clear he was unhappy with their 'leadership' and support.

local troops almost immediately, at a time when they were the only jungle-ready troops available to him.

All the same, a land invasion seemed unlikely. Even the Japanese wanted to attack from the sea and, in May, another invasion force set off and stealthily crept around the coast to Port Moresby. What the Japanese commanders did not know was that the Japanese Fleet code (JN-25) had been broken, so naval messages could be read by decoders in Melbourne.

The Japanese army codes were not broken until 1943, but it was the naval codes that mattered most. The Japanese army had to be transported on ships. Whatever the Japanese planned, the Allies knew where they were going and how many transport craft they had.

Most people who have studied the World War II period agree that General MacArthur was excellent at publicity and politics, but had limited combat experience.

Luckily, the US military had many brilliant leaders and that included US Admiral Chester Nimitz. Nimitz had sent bombers to Lae to halt the earlier invasion plan and he did not stop at that.

On 4 May, the Japanese command sent a fleet of eleven transports loaded with troops out of Rabaul, protected by destroyers, cruisers and an aircraft carrier. They were headed for Port Moresby, where the carrier's planes and the cruisers' guns would soften the town before the troops stormed ashore and wiped out any remaining opposition.

Armed with this knowledge through decoded intercepted messages from the Japanese, Nimitz immediately positioned his ships in the Coral Sea to stop the Japanese advance. Previously, naval battles were fought by ships with guns, but the Coral Sea was the first naval battle where the opposing ships never saw each other. Instead of the ships shooting at each other, all the strikes were made by aircraft launched from aircraft carriers.

Today, we celebrate the time as the victorious Battle of the Coral Sea, and it was a victory, but a costly one. The US lost more ships than the Japanese navy, but the Japanese losses included the only aircraft carrier with the transports.

Without the carrier, the invading troops had no air cover and their fleet could easily be sunk. They had no choice but to turn back.

Nankai Shitai

The Imperial Army's plan to capture Port Moresby by sea was crushed with their defeat in the Battle of the Coral Sea and the Battle of Midway in June. In June 1942, Lieutenant General Hyakutake Harukichi was ordered to rethink taking Port Moresby. Hyakutake chose Major General Horii Tomitaro to the lead the offensive and the force was called 'Nankai Shitai' (South Seas Detachment). The infantry's job was to report whether the main force of the detachment could feasibly land on the northern coast of New Guinea, launching from their nearby base at Rabaul and capture Moresby from an overland position.

One reason for the change was that the Japanese also had internal political trouble. Leaders of the Japanese army and navy did not see eye to eye; the navy was unwilling to risk its ships to help the army mount another attack from the sea.

Because the naval commanders were uncooperative with the army, it made sense for the Japanese army to land on the northern side of Papua, just as Rowell had predicted in early February. The idea was that they would swoop across the island, taking Port Moresby from the rear.

Secure the Kokoda airstrip

On the Allied side, nobody was sent to look at the Kokoda Track. There were no detailed maps, and little was known about the track conditions. Allied Headquarters in Brisbane was aware, however, of an airstrip at Kokoda. On 29 June, Blamey ordered Major General Morris in Port Moresby to send some men over the mountains to secure the airstrip, so it could be used as a forward base to attack the Japanese in other areas. He made no mention of any Japanese plans for an invasion of Port Moresby over that route, even though he must have known about them through the interception of decoded Japanese messages.

Fighting the land
'From its beginning, the New Guinea campaign has defied comparison with any other part of this or the last great war... Beyond new military roads stretched native footpads. Beyond again were tumbled rock and strangling jungle. To fight the enemy was nothing compared with the conquest of the land itself.'
— Soldier VX17681, *Soldiering On* published by Australian War Memorial, Canberra, ACT 1942.

Even at the end of June 1942, five months after General Rowell had warned of a possible attack over the Owen Stanley Range and six weeks after the Japanese plans had been uncovered in their coded signals, it seemed nobody was concerned about the risk of an invasion over the mountains. So why were troops finally sent there?

Maybe it was just a case of good luck. General MacArthur's major goal was to chase the Japanese out of the Philippines. Taking Rabaul was a step back to the Philippines, and he wanted an airstrip at Dobodura, on New Guinea's north coast, but only as a base to take Rabaul.

MacArthur wanted the liberation of the Philippines. He requested an Australian force to guard the airstrip at Kokoda. Their job was to help protect the planned airstrip at Dobodura.

Imagine you are there...

We all lost weight working down on the coast. I mean, most days, it was a hundred degrees on the Fahrenheit scale we used then. Plus the humidity was always close to 100 per cent, and we were doing hard physical work. Forget about fighting a war, it felt like I was working in a chain gang.

One day, I went swimming down at Ela Beach and found I'd lost so much fat that I sank when I breathed out. In salt water! I mentioned this to the doc, and he said it wasn't unusual. He also said I'd need to be careful swimming in fresh water, because I would sink even quicker!

Drink more beer, he said, eat more meat, and get some condition. Easy for him to say, when there was no beer, and the meat was mostly horse— well, that's what we reckoned it was!

After complaining so long about the heat of Moresby, it is weird going up into the mountains. We left the blinding glare of Port Moresby and moved into a landscape that is green and damp and gloomy. There are odd noises in the trees and on the ground — noises I couldn't account for — that could drive you to distraction if you let them.

It is cold at night. After the heat of Moresby, it is a shock to the system. I complained about the cold the first night and my mate Harry reckoned I was never happy. Who would be? I just want to be home. Losing that layer of fat under my skin has meant I feel the cold even more than I should. Some nights I dream of sweating under the heat of the Port Moresby sky once more.

When we landed at Moresby they gave us each a gun, but our tents and extra clothes weren't unloaded for another ten days. Some silly bugger had packed them all first. We didn't even have things to eat with — no tins or plates or forks. There were only a few mossie nets and you could forget the quinine.

Those damn mossies. They hung around day and night — I gave up trying to kill them.

So here I am up the Track. There aren't as many mossies up here. Thank God for small mercies.

Papuan Infantry Battalion

Before the militia arrived in Port Moresby, a battalion known as the Papuan Infantry Battalion (PIB) had been raised in late 1940 in Papua and New Guinea. This battalion was the first to encounter the Japanese on the track, although when the Japanese landed in Papua they were shot at briefly by a few men from the New Guinea Volunteer Rifles.

The PIB consisted of Australian officers and senior NCOs, with privates and other NCOs drawn from police volunteers and men from a number of regions including the Kokoda area. These were people who knew the land well — how to live in and off it. By February 1941 there were three companies and the battalion had 16 Europeans and 285 Pacific Islands personnel.

At first, the PIB were also set to work building roads, unloading ships and even quarrying but with time they received some military training. When the new militia battalions arrived in January 1942, the PIB became active as a military force. In February, General Morris sent a PIB platoon out to patrol the coast near Buna. On 6 June 1942, the whole of the PIB (30 officers and 280 men) were sent out to patrol an area from Awala — a day and a half from the north coast — to points about five days' march north-east and south-east of where the track hit the coast.

Chapter 3
Up the Track

General Blamey finally ordered General Morris to send troops to Kokoda on 29 June, but the troops did not actually leave until 7 July.

With no urgency, a small army unit set off to Kokoda. Instead of a 20-minute plane ride, the soldiers were ordered to walk for eight days, carrying their equipment, arms, ammunition, food and anything else they needed. Kokoda is only about three days' walk from the sea on the north side of New Guinea, so a small lugger was sent around the coast to deliver extra supplies.

The first party was just one company of the 39th Battalion — Sam Templeton's B Company — which consisted of 94 officers and men, as well as some PIB troops and about 120 carriers to help bring equipment over the mountains. The group were referred to as Maroubra Force. Each soldier carried an official 18 kg, but with a rifle weighing 4 kg and shared battalion equipment, each soldier's load was closer to 27 kg. This is not too hard to carry if you are fit, but that was the limit for any work that involved climbing steep hills. More importantly, once they got to Kokoda, the soldiers would need fresh supplies.

Maroubra Force

Army structures work on regular patterns. A battalion, a brigade or a division will all be made up of troops of the same kind, for example all AIF or all militia. When a mixed force is set up, it needs a short name. Maroubra Force was the name given to the mixed troops of the 39th Battalion and the Papuan Infantry Battalion.

Later, when the 53rd Battalion came up with the AIF 2/14th and 2/16th battalions, they also became part of Maroubra Force, and so did the 2/27th Battalion. So at one point, Maroubra Force was a single militia company and a few PIB patrol groups, but eventually it included more units than a normal brigade, even if many of the men in it had been killed or badly wounded.

Maroubra Force saw action again at the end of 1942 and early 1943, when the Japanese were forced out of the Buna and Gona areas on New Guinea's north coast, where the whole Kokoda campaign had begun, some six months earlier.

Kokoda conditions

Without a survey of the track, nobody in command could begin to understand what the conditions were. To them the track was just a line drawn on the map, beginning at Port Moresby on the south coast and ending at the north coast. Only a dozen Europeans had ever walked over it and some of those were probably already in the jungle, as part of an Australian guerrilla force that was attacking the Japanese near Lae.

There was at least one man who knew the track, and knew it well. Bert Kienzle was a gold miner who struck it rich in New Guinea and then used the proceeds to start a rubber plantation at Yodda, about 10 km from the airstrip at Kokoda. Kienzle was a big man, described in those days as 'six foot two and 18 stone' (about 190 cm and 115 kg). He was born in Fiji, but he had been in New Guinea since 1927, so he knew the local people and understood them, and they knew and trusted him.

In March 1942, Kienzle was told to round up some of the 'deserters', the contract labourers who had left Port Moresby when the bombing started, and bring them back to Port Moresby. He must have been persuasive, because soon after he turned up at Koitaki with 64 men. It had taken them seven days to walk to Port Moresby from Kokoda.

If anybody had bothered to ask him, Kienzle could have explained the track in detail. But Kienzle, who was now part of the army, was only a lieutenant, and important people were unlikely to waste valuable time talking to a junior officer.

If asked, Kienzle would have explained that there was no single 'track', no clear path to follow. Instead, there was a network of paths through the jungle, maintained by the tread of bare feet as people moved from village to village. He could have told them it was not a simple walk up one side of a mountain range before the track ran down the other side to the sea. Whichever set of paths you followed, the Kokoda Track was a roller-coaster ride of desperate climbs and terrifying drops — up and down, and up and down, over and over again.

The track began as a narrow dusty road in Port Moresby, climbing to the Sogeri Plateau after about 40 kilometres of rough driving. Troops were driven by truck to the end of this narrow road, but they had to walk the rest of the way.

The group met up with Kienzle at the start of the track. Rather than waste time trying to build a road, Kienzle had sent his labourers ahead to set up staging camps and used the rest as carriers. By the time the soldiers began walking they were well away from the sweaty tropical coast. The nights were cold enough for them to need a sweater. They had a hard slog ahead of them, before they got over the Range. The road finally petered out after making its way across the plateau, to be replaced by a faint narrow track that disappeared into the jungle.

Building any road past Sogeri would have required bulldozers. Only four-wheel-drive trucks with chains on their wheels would be able to drive on the road, and only then if a 'corduroy road' was laid. This meant chopping down trees to make logs as long as the road was wide, then placing them side-by-side, giving the appearance of a giant corduroy.

Ignoring the realities, General Morris looked at the map and told Bert Kienzle in late June to take a thousand labourers out and build a road over the mountains within eight weeks. It took very little time for Kienzle to conclude that any army wanting to get over the range had two choices. Either they had to be air-lifted, or they had to walk, carrying and hauling their food, their weapons and ammunition, their shelter, their medical supplies and anything else they needed. It was never going to be easy, and there was no chance of ever doing it in vehicles. He could see a better way to use the labourers than to make a road to nowhere.

The stores problem

The tale of Kokoda is a tale of military strategy. It is about the difficulty of maintaining extended supply lines — especially in mountainous terrain in a tropical jungle serviced by only a few tracks.

The normal method of travelling in New Guinea in 1942 was to walk to your destination with a long line of carriers. There were clear rules for the use of these

Soldiers clearing the track to make a road.

carriers. Standard contracts limited the time of such service, guaranteed that workers would be returned to their villages at the end of the time, and laid down pay rates and the food and clothing that would be issued.

Loads were usually carried in metal patrol boxes. These added to the weight, but they kept things dry and could be locked to prevent stealing. They had metal handles that you could slip a pole through, so two men could carry it between them.

While the carriers could be fined or gaoled for failing to work as agreed, the rules protected them and were seen as fair. There were about 45,000 labourers in Papua New Guinea in 1942. While some labourers happily volunteered, most were conscripted from their local village.

The carriers were organised in village groups. The village policeman often went along as a sort of 'head man', and one man in the team would be the cook. The cook was in charge of the carriers' rations. Every week, each carrier received 8 pounds (3.6 kg) of rice, 3 pounds (1.4 kg) of flour, 2 pounds (900 grams) of biscuits (hard bread), 1 pound (450 grams) each of meat, fish and sugar, a box of matches, some salt and soap and two sticks of trade tobacco — evil smelling tarry stuff that was favoured by locals, both islanders and Europeans.

A carrier who took nothing but food would eat all of his rations in 13 days and if he carried food for a soldier there was just six and a half days' supply for both soldier and carrier. To get further along the track, more carriers were needed at the start of the track, carrying food forward for others to eat as they carried more supplies onto the next stage. This ended up as a chain of carriers, hauling food forward. But food was not the only concern.

Ammunition, equipment, medical stores, telephone wire, cooking pots, tools, spare parts, nails, maps, notepaper, mail and dozens of other items all had to be carried on the backs of men. Walking the track to the Kokoda village took eight days from the road near Port Moresby. Using carriers to deliver the supplies for a whole army was impossible. Ideally, planes were needed to drop food and equipment, but at the start of the fighting, planes were just not available.

Kienzle understood that building the road was an impossibility. Instead he used his time to set up stages and organised the carriers who only travelled one stage, then returned — all in the name of good morale.

B Company made good time. They reached Kokoda on 15 July and found everything peaceful. They began to settle in, but their peace was about to be rudely shattered.

First contact

On the night of 22 July, a patrol from the PIB saw Japanese troops landing at Gona on the northern

Livestock Carriers
Horses, brumbies and mules were used at the start of the track. They were hard to manage on the narrow track but worth the effort, for each animal carried 160 pounds — as much as four carriers. The catch was that they, like carriers, needed food as well as other supplies.

coast of New Guinea. They could not judge the strength of the Japanese force, but there were between 1500 and 2000 Japanese soldiers ashore. The invasion had begun. The patrol's task was to get away and report and this is what they did.

On 23 July, PIB troops engaged the Japanese in the late afternoon near Awala — a day and a half along the track — but the Japanese had machine guns and mortars to fight an enemy armed only with rifles, so the PIB troops withdrew. As the PIB left, they dropped trees across the track to slow any vehicles, and they hauled out the log bridges that might have made it easier for the Japanese to advance.

As they moved up the track, the PIB met with a platoon from the 39th Battalion coming down to collect stores from the lugger, and handed over to them. After that, the European officers of the PIB patrol merged into Maroubra Force while some of the islanders 'went bush' and didn't take part in the fighting until much later. The PIB now operated more or less as a part of the 39th or they harassed the Japanese from the jungle.

All that stood in the way of the Japanese advance was one platoon from B Company of the 39th Battalion and their allies from the PIB.

The Japanese landing had been reported to Port Moresby by radio and, on 23 July, General Morris was told to send the rest of the 39th Battalion over the range to Kokoda. C Company left that day to follow B Company, and the battalion's commander, Lieutenant Colonel Owen, was flown to Kokoda airstrip to take charge. Owen was an experienced AIF officer who had escaped from Rabaul, but he had only taken command on 7 July, the day that B Company left for Kokoda.

The rest of the 39th Battalion was told to prepare to join the fight. From Australia, General Morris was advised that there would be a delivery of 50 tons of munitions and equipment to Kokoda by plane,

Lieutenant Colonel W. T. Owen
William Taylor Owen was born in Nagambie, Victoria, in May 1905. He worked as a bank officer before the war and enlisted in the Australian Imperial Forces (AIF) in 1940. Owen was one of 1400 soldiers involved in defending Rabaul against the Japanese in January 1942 and was one of the 400 survivors to leave Rabaul safely. Owen assumed command of the 39th Battalion on 7 July 1942.

but that the troops would need to walk. That same day, the single platoon from B Company retreated back past Wairopi (the name referred to a wire rope bridge over the fast stream). Once across, they cut the bridge down to slow any Japanese advance. On 26 July, one platoon from D Company was flown in by two flights to Kokoda village. More of D Company flew to Kokoda on 28 July. By then the Japanese were close to the airstrip and the American pilots refused to land, fearing their planes would be attacked on the ground. From now on, all reinforcements would have to come in the hard way, via foot, and so would most of the supplies.

Fighting below Kokoda

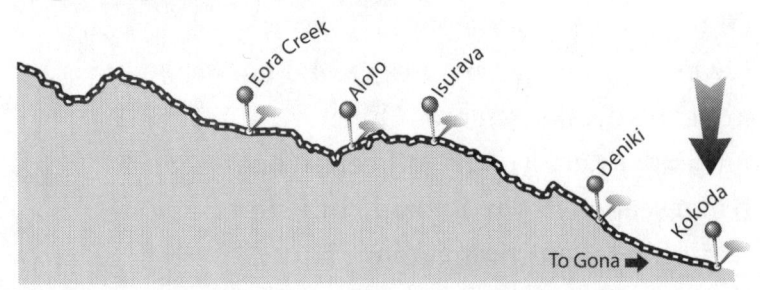

Kokoda village sits about 400 metres above sea level on the northern side of the Owen Stanley Range. In 1942 there was an airstrip near the village on which planes could land to resupply troops fighting on the north coast. About two hours away, the gold mine at Yodda had a strip as well. These were just patches of open ground where the worst gullies and snags had been filled or cleared, but bush pilots knew how to land on them. The Kokoda village held no value but its airstrip was a strategic location worth defending.

It is worth remembering that the decoded signals intercepted by the Allies showed very clearly that the Japanese landing was the start of an attempt to cross the Owen Stanley Range and then take Port Moresby from the rear. If the Australians at Kokoda had understood this, what followed might have been very different. As it was, local commanders made decisions based on the belief that the Japanese wanted to capture and use the Kokoda airstrip, although the Japanese never used it at any time.

The Japanese army also had strange ideas about the track over the mountains. They had planned to build a road all the way to Port Moresby and, on paper, their plans looked promising. On the coast there was a track that vehicles could use, and then a narrower track that the Japanese could travel along on bicycles. Bicycles had worked well on the level tracks in Malaya, but they were less useful on the steep and muddy mountains of the Owen Stanley Range.

It takes three days to walk to Kokoda from the north coast, but the first of the Japanese forces covered half the distance quickly, because there were tracks suitable for bicycles and vehicles. After that, though, they came to very different country, where ravines filled with rushing water had to be crossed. The Japanese engineers could not get a road through this in a hurry, and the advance slowed as they tested the opposition, to see how strong it was.

This was probably the time when the Japanese had the greatest advantage. They would always outnumber the Australians, but now there were just a handful of untrained young men with limited equipment between them and the Japanese objective. If the attackers had pushed on, they would have been victorious, but for some reason, the cautious Japanese commanders held back.

Days 1 to 3, 25 to 27 July 1942 Templeton killed

On 25 July, two platoons of B Company exchanged fire with the Japanese between Wairopi and Gorari, as the Japanese moved towards Kokoda. By 26 July, the Australians were taking casualties, and running low on ammunition, but they were getting closer to base, and had some hope that reinforcements would be there soon.

The Japanese troops used a pattern of attack that they would use throughout the campaign. Human waves would advance up the track, absorbing any losses by pushing more troops into the attack. At the same time, other Japanese troops would slip off the track into the jungle on each side, and work their way past the fight, to come onto the track behind the defenders. Once they had cut the track behind their enemy, the Japanese could stop any reinforcements getting through, and they could also attack the defenders from behind.

On 26 July, the first troops from 16 Platoon, D Company, came forward after they flew in to Kokoda. By then, the Australians had withdrawn to Oivi, not far from Kokoda, which made it easier for D Company to join the fighting. Reinforcements were expected. The problem was that these fresh troops would not be expecting to find a Japanese ambush on the track.

Sam Templeton went back up the track, planning to warn the new D Company troops to watch out for this trap, but he was too late. Some Japanese soldiers were already on the track, a burst of machine-gun fire was heard, and Templeton was never seen again. It was later reported that the Japanese believed they were facing a thousand Australians, and there has been speculation that the wounded Templeton may have told them this before he died, or was killed.

Several groups of men became lost in the withdrawal but later participated in the fighting at Isurava. PIB officer, Major Watson, and the platoon commanders steadied the remaining soldiers, and the group made an orderly retreat down off the track into a creek. Lance Corporal Sanopa of the PIB led the troops along the creek to the village of Fila, and on to the village of Deniki, south of Kokoda. Sanopa saved two platoons from being wiped out that day, giving the Australians a large enough force to continue fighting. Sanopa was never awarded a medal, and very little information about him is available. It seems likely that he was killed at some stage during the campaign, but in late July 1942 he was a brilliant guide.

Back at the airstrip, stragglers from Oivi arrived at about 2 a.m. on 5 July, and reported the situation to Lieutenant Colonel Owen. At this time, Sanopa was still leading the rest of the troops to Fila, so Owen had to assume the worst: that those troops had all been killed. He had too few troops left to defend the airstrip, so he ordered the men to burn or destroy all the stores. The following morning, the remaining 50 troops moved back up the track to Deniki, where Sanopa's group of about 30 men had already arrived from Oivi.

Imagine talking to a Brigadier...

'Thank you for taking time to see me, Brigadier.'
   'Not at all, not at all.'
   'I was just wondering if I could get a comment from you regarding General Blamey. I have heard a few grumblings lately—'
   'You know something? Troops always say the same sort of things about their commanders. Always have done. Probably always will. The troops say that commanders hide under cover. But they don't understand the strain that they experience — that any leader experiences. Whether it's winning a battle or winning a war, every commander needs strong nerves, quick wits, and an ability to see the bigger picture.'
   'So you think General Blamey sees the bigger picture, sir?'
   'I won't discuss Blamey. Let me give you an example. When General So-and-so knows that there is a battle to be fought, he and his staff need to think about what forces and resources are available. They need to think as well about the consequences if those troops are defeated. Sometimes a few troops are sacrificed so that a larger number can survive. Often, a general has to choose which units will be sent, and which will stay behind.'
   'That wouldn't make them very popular?'
   'Indeed. And of course, senior generals command more

troops, so in reality they need to send more men to their death. They are also engaged in more battles. Generals have to source the equipment the troops need. They also need to keep the respect of those below them, so that when they send men into what looks like a hopeless situation, the soldiers will keep fighting, and win through.'

'So leaders are attacked by those ranked below them?'

'And those above. If they don't win enough battles, they will be dismissed. If too many men to die under their command, they will be dismissed. In most cases, there will be other people at the same rank ready to step into their shoes.'

'In other words, you wouldn't like to be in General Blamey's shoes?'

'Listen — it's easy to poke fun at generals. They're easy targets. Maybe they have very healthy egos, but they wouldn't have risen to the top ranks without them! You can be sure they wouldn't have attained their position if they weren't also pretty darn good at what they do. Generals get criticised if they take risks and get it wrong, or if they are too timid and get it wrong. They can send troops off to one location, when they are desperately needed in another and a whole war can be lost.'

'It sounds like you're happy to be well out of this war, Sir.'

'Off the record? I made three risky decisions during World War I. Twice I was lucky, because my troops got out with some casualties, but we won. The third time, I was very close to being retired in disgrace, before the enemy blundered and gave us the battle. So go easy when you're looking to blame someone. War is madness. Unless you're there, unless you're in charge, you have no idea what Blamey is going through.'

'Is he good?'

'Some people say he's brilliant but a bastard; I say he's a bastard, but brilliant.'

'Is he always brilliant?'

'Good Heavens! Is that the time? Must go!'

Chapter 4
Kokoda and Deniki

Days 4 to 5, 28 and 29 July Fighting for Kokoda

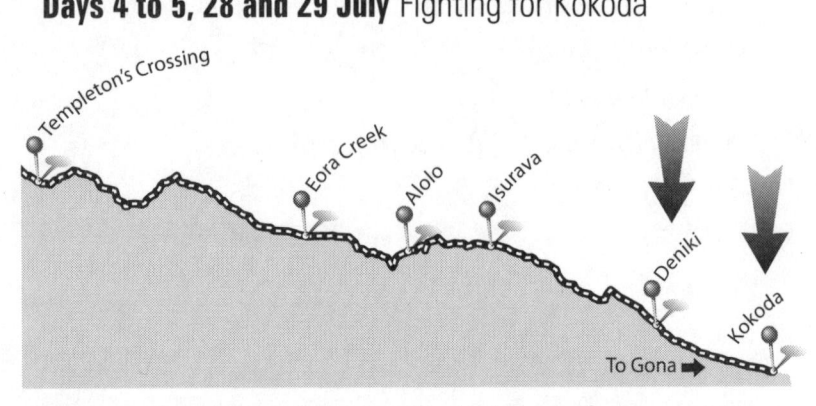

Lieutenant Colonel Owen had already informed Port Moresby by radio that he had abandoned the airstrip. He said that with so few men left, it could not be defended, and he could really only hope to hold the track. It would have been better to hold the airstrip and have reinforcements and supplies flown in, but he was a realist. Then he received some new information that meant he needed to rethink the situation.

On the night of 26 July, six men from B and D companies left Oivi at midnight. They made their way through rough country, reached Kokoda on the 27th, and slept there that night. When they reached Deniki on the morning of 28 July, they told Owen that the Japanese had not yet taken the airstrip. It might still be used by the Australians.

The commanders in Australia knew from decoding the Japanese naval messages that the attack was aimed at Port Moresby. In spite of this, they allowed the local commanders to keep thinking that the main target was the airstrip at Kokoda. Because the local commanders were given wrong information, two of them made the same wrong decision within a few days of each other, and tried to hold the airstrip.

Lieutenant Colonel Owen was the first.

He moved his troops back around the airstrip on 28 July, and then radioed Port Moresby to tell them the airstrip was open. He asked for mortars and more troops, set his troops to defend against any Japanese attack, and waited hopefully. Before long, two DC3 aircraft appeared, and his men went out to clear the strip of the obstacles they had put there to stop any Japanese planes from landing.

The planes had another platoon from D Company, but no mortars. Unfortunately, the American pilots could see ground activity and mistakenly believed they were Japanese troops and believed the planes would be fired on if they landed. Captain Max Bidstrup was on one of the planes and asked the pilots to land, but they refused and flew back to Port Moresby. The platoon would have to walk in.

That night, back in Port Moresby, Bidstrup was visited by General Morris. Bidstrup told the general the militia needed mortars, saying there was a lot of open ground where they could be used.

'Rot, boy! Bloody rot!' roared General Morris. 'The mortars would burst in the tree tops.'

And that was the end, for the time being, of any issue of that most portable form of artillery to the front line troops on the Kokoda Track.

Bidstrup extracted an effective revenge when a truck pulled up at his company headquarters the night before D Company headed up the track. Where, asked the driver, was Brigade HQ? Calmly, the captain asked why he wanted to know, and the driver said he had six Bren guns, highly effective light machine guns, to deliver. Bidstrup assured the driver that he was in the right place, and signed for the weapons, knowing that D Company would be way up the track before anybody realised the 'error'.

Back on the ground just north of Kokoda, at 2 a.m. on day 5, the Japanese army fired at the Australians with their mortars and heavy machine guns. Given that the Japanese had about 1500 troops, it should have been all over that day.

The diggers faced the first wave of enemy troops and found themselves unprepared for the sheer force of numbers against them. Still, they caused considerable casualties amongst the Japanese. But whenever one Japanese soldier fell, there was another to replace him.

Still the Japanese pressed forward. Looking at the figures on paper, the Japanese army should have been streaming over the Owen Stanley Range to Port Moresby. The Australians were probably outnumbered five to one, and outgunned as well.

Lieutenant Colonel Owen deployed his men around the Kokoda plateau in hopes that they could hold out against the Japanese. The Australians answered the attack as well as they could with rifles and grenades, but it was an unequal battle. With only 77 sleep-deprived soldiers left, Owen urged his troops on with encouraging words and recognition of their bravery. He was shot, reportedly, while throwing a hand grenade at the enemy.

Owen was rushed to the Regimental Aid Post, or RAP, where Doc Vernon could offer no treatment but to make Owen comfortable as he died.

Pull back to Deniki

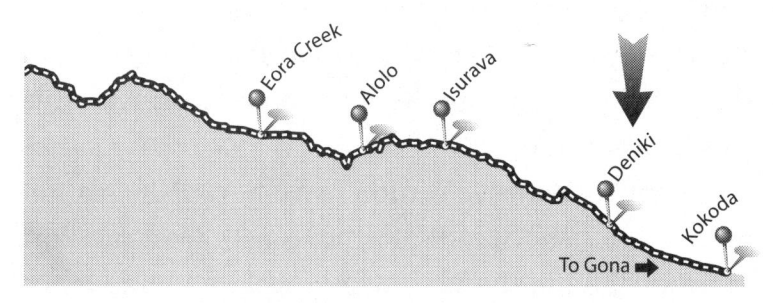

In the end, the Australians had to pull back and take refuge at Deniki. They had taken a calculated risk, to try to regain Kokoda airstrip, but the bad judgement of two American pilots meant the Australian troops gained nothing and lost a great deal. They remained at Deniki until 4 August, while the Japanese began to build up their numbers down the track at Kokoda.

Once again, the Japanese forces made the mistake of waiting for reinforcements before they advanced. There is some speculation that Templeton lied about the strength of the Australians and that this was reinforced by the fact that the Australians seemed like a much larger force.

At this time, the only thing stopping the Japanese from reaching Port Moresby were a few hundred Australian militia.

The 39th were fighting like tigers.

Doc Vernon

A nervous sentry almost shot the strange stork-like figure that loomed out of the mist at Deniki. The figure seemed to be wearing shorts (on closer inspection, the sentry saw they were rolled-up trousers), and had a blue sweater tied around his neck and a couple of slings loaded with instruments and dressings. This was Doc Vernon.

Captain Geoffrey Vernon was a rubber planter from Daru, an island off the coast, west of Port Moresby. Before the war, when explorers, traders or gold prospectors got sick, they would head for Daru and put themselves in Doc's capable hands. He was typical of the tough characters found in Papua and New Guinea in those days.

Vernon, a tall thin man with a lined face, suffered

from recurring malaria symptoms. He was a veteran of World War I, where a close shell blast at Gallipoli had made him extremely deaf. In 1916 he won the Military Cross for conspicuous gallantry. When the war began, he was over 60 and too old to fight, said the authorities, who ordered him back to Australia. Vernon ignored that, and set to work being useful. He joined the PIB in February 1942 and established a hospital at Ilolo, located at the start of the Kokoda Track, at the Port Moresby end.

By June 1942, he was looking after the health of the carriers along the track. He'd used this as an excuse to move up to Deniki, knowing there was fighting going on and his skills might be needed.

Days 11 to 14, 4 to 7 August Regain the Airstrip

Major Watson of the PIB was left in control for a few days until Major Allan Cameron, the Brigade Major of 30th Brigade, arrived on 4 August with more of the 39th Battalion. Cameron, an AIF officer who had escaped from Rabaul with Owen, was a man given to harsh judgements. He had heard of the retreat from Kokoda and decided that the soldiers of B Company were cowards.

Cameron sent patrols out on 5 August, but the patrols failed to locate the Japanese. The result was that Cameron made a mistake and under-estimated the Japanese strength, which allowed him to make a second mistake — the same one Owen had made. Cameron elected to fight over a useless airstrip. By now Cameron had all five companies of the 39th Battalion with him, but he sent the despised B Company back up the track, and held E Company in reserve while he set about trying to take the airstrip from the Japanese.

Keeping soldiers back from the battle for the airstrip was probably a lucky mistake, because it meant Cameron would still have some fighting troops left when his plan to take the Kokoda airstrip failed. He started with 41 officers and 478 soldiers, but ended up with many fewer, and all for nothing.

Cameron believed his job was to take control of the airstrip, both for the long term needs of fighting a war, and as a way of getting reinforcements and supplies.

The Japanese considered the airstrip as just one more obstacle to overcome on their way to Port Moresby. The airstrip turned out to be useless to the Australians, who got no troop reinforcements, while the only supplies dropped at the strip landed among Japanese troops.

So Cameron's plan to try to hold the airstrip was risky but understandable. The plan was for Captain Dean's C Company to move in along the main track and break through the weak Japanese defences.

Captain Bidstrup's D Company was to set an ambush to take out any Japanese reinforcements coming up from Oivi, further down on the coastward side of the track. And Captain Symington's A Company would move to the airstrip along an apparently unused track which they had found while patrolling.

By this time, the Australians had learned to recognise Japanese bootprints, which looked as though they had two toes. The track seemed to be completely clear of such prints, suggesting that Japanese patrols had not yet found it. The track would be a back door, a way to get onto the airstrip before they were seen.

The D Company ambush was successful, with nearly 50 Japanese killed, and as many more wounded. But the Japanese army had more soldiers in reserve — soldiers who now knew the location of D Company, so Bidstrup withdrew his troops, just before night closed in. They were supposed to join up with A Company, but they had no way of knowing where A Company was, or even if they had made it to the airstrip.

One of the platoons of D Company was separated in the fighting, and took two days to circle around and get back to Deniki.

C Company walked straight into an ambush. Captain Dean was among those killed, and the company had to turn back, leaving just one company near the airstrip.

If D Company had tried to push through to the airstrip as ordered, they would have walked into the same ambush.

Once again, the Australians were lucky.

Day 15, 8 August Arrival of the 21st Brigade, 2nd AIF in Port Moresby

Meanwhile, 3000 men of the 21st Brigade 2/AIF arrived in Port Moresby on 8 August. Their arrival transformed the Seven-mile Strip into a bustling military base. They were armed with the latest firearms and an assuredness in their ability to wipe out the enemy. They still wore the khaki uniform, with light-coloured webbing that had been bleached by the sun. Their packs and equipment weighed over 27kg.

Each rifleman carried two grenades, a rifle, and about 100 to 150 rounds of ammunition. Then there were the shared items. The AIF soldiers had a 2-inch mortar and a 3-inch mortar and mortar bombs to fit. Then there were Bren guns, each with ten magazines, tommy guns, magazines and extra loose rounds. Each battalion had five carrier-loads (100 kg) of medical equipment and cooking gear, along with two picks and two axes, while each section had a machete and a spade, six telephones and six radio sets.

After several days of jungle combat training, they gathered at Itiki where they received orders from their new commander, Brigadier Arnold Potts. They were to go up the track and relieve the soldiers of the 39th Battalion. Because of the shortage of supplies, though, they did not reach the 39th Battalion until day 33, 26 August.

Days 15 to 17, 8 to 10 August A Company at Kokoda Symington's A Company from the 39th Battalion set out from Deniki, each man with 100 rounds of ammunition, two grenades, and food for two days. They had no way of knowing what was happening with the other companies, but Lance Corporal Sanopa led them along the disused track to a position where they could hold the airstrip and fire on any Japanese reinforcements that got past or around the D Company ambush. There seemed to be only a small group of Japanese soldiers in view, and when fired on, these soldiers ran for it, so very few shots were fired.

Kokoda airstrip was now in Australian hands. All that was needed now was to call in the aircraft, but the radio was with Cameron, back at Deniki. B Company Sergeant Major Jim Cowey, walked out to the middle of the airstrip and fired a Verey Light (a type of flare, shot off from a pistol) which Cameron had suggested as the best way to signal that the airstrip was taken. Nobody at Deniki saw it go up.

Looking back, it was probably just as well the signal was not seen, because it would have led to Cameron sending C and D companies back to the airstrip again. The Australian force was outnumbered at least five to one. The Japanese had better arms and far better supplies of ammunition. If the Australians had been bunched at the airstrip, many more of them would have been killed.

Guns On the Track
.303, Bren and Thompson

.303
The main weapon used by soldiers in World War II was the Lee Enfield .303-inch calibre rifle. Developed in the early 1900s and slightly modified later, the '.303' had a magazine holding ten rounds, operated by a bolt which cleared the old cartridge case and pushed a new live round into the breech. It was simple and accurate, and any soldier could fire off 15 aimed rounds in a minute. It was heavy, weighing just over 4 kilograms, but it was highly reliable.

Bren
The Bren gun was a light machine gun used ammunition loaded in magazines of 30 rounds. It weighed just over 10 kg, so it was usually fired from a lying position, with the front of the barrel resting on two legs. On rapid fire, the 30 rounds would be sent off in just under four seconds.

Thompson
The Thompson submachine gun or 'tommy gun' was developed late in World War I as a 'trench broom', and then became popular with gangsters in America during Prohibition in the 1930s. Weighing just under 5 kilograms, it fired a 0.45 round, and it carried between 20 and 100 rounds in a box or

drum magazine, and proved extremely useful in jungle patrol work, usually with a smaller box magazine, because the big drums had a nasty habit of 'jamming'.

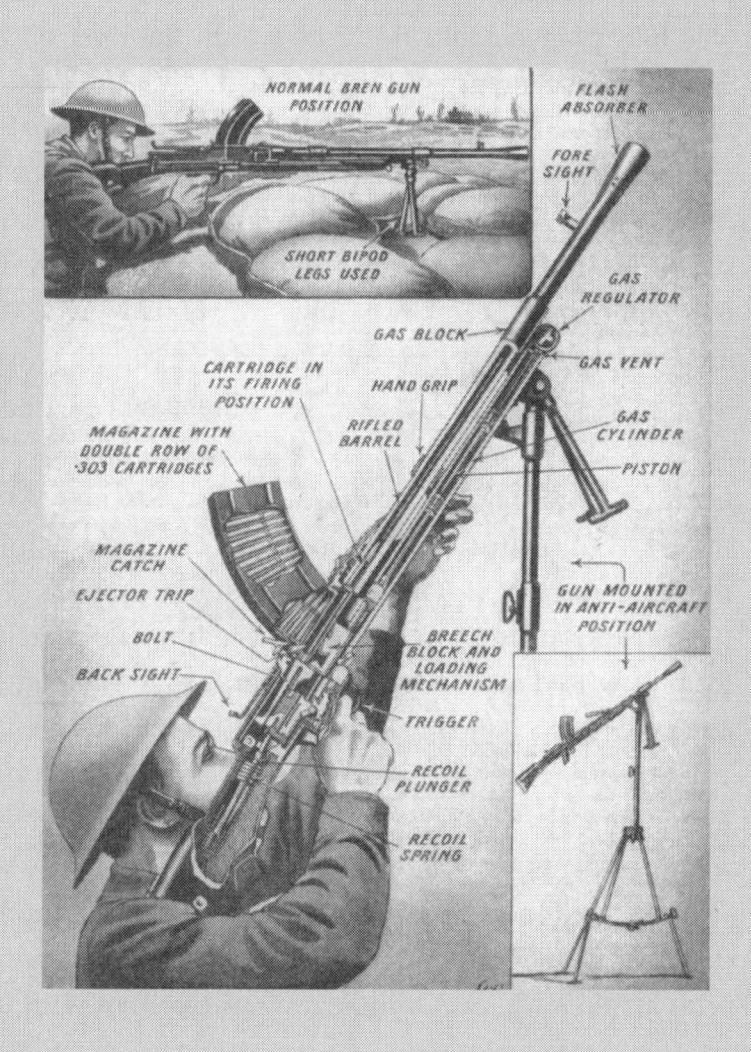

As it was, enough soldiers survived to hold off the Japanese attack over the next few weeks.

In the middle of day 16, Sunday 9 August, there were two attacks on the airstrip by around 200 troops, and a messenger was sent to tell Cameron the Japanese had taken the strip. When he heard this, Cameron called for support from Port Moresby, and was told planes could not arrive until the next day. This, he countered, would be too late. On Sunday afternoon, about 300 Japanese attacked, and then another attack was launched at 10.30 p.m.

On day 17, 10 August, Monday morning, an Allied plane flew over the Kokoda airstrip, sighted the Japanese troops, and flew away. This would have been a good time to provide air attacks on the Japanese forces. Instead, the pilot just reported Japanese activity, which meant there was no chance of fresh troops or supplies being landed at Kokoda. All the effort to secure the airstrip had been a waste, but the Australians had not finished paying the price.

In the tropics, there is almost no twilight. The switch from light to dark is very sudden, and as the evening of day 17 approached, 300 Japanese stormed the area. The Australians were running out of ammunition. Symington had set a 7.30 p.m. deadline to receive reinforcements.

The deadline came and went and Symington decided to get his company out of the area. A man with a rifle and ammunition can fight, a man with a rifle and no ammunition should withdraw and get more ammunition to fight again.

Even now, there was a steadying influence as the Australian troops eased their way out.

Day 18, 11 August Jim Cowey Saves the Day
People who write about the 39th usually refer to the battalion as boys, but there were older men among them as well, and one of the oldest was a coolheaded 52-year-old veteran of World War I, Jim Cowey, who was B company's sergeant major. As Symington's troops withdrew, Cowey stayed behind with two tommy gunners, who apparently appointed themselves as his bodyguard.

The 'tommy gun' or Thompson Light Machine Gun was a hand-held weapon that fired heavy (0.45 calibre) bullets or 'slugs' at high speed. The weapon had been issued to the 39th Battalion as they left to walk up the track, and they learned how to use it on their trek to Kokoda. It was an awesome weapon whenever an enemy was concentrated in a group and it had the advantage of being portable.

Cowey's work that night and on the trek back probably saved 15 lives. First, he rounded up the stragglers. One of these men suggested making a run for it, because the Japanese were swarming through the area, looking under huts and dropping grenades in the weapons pits, the small trenches the Australians had been using. Cowey shook his head and said, 'We'll walk out, they don't know who we are.' And so they walked across the airstrip in single file, over a bridge that crossed Madi Creek, and then he led them into the dense scrub that lay beyond. Cowey had realised that any Japanese soldiers who saw them in the dark would assume that the Australians were Japanese soldiers searching for an elusive enemy.

Once they were safe in the scrub, the tired Australian soldiers lay down to sleep, while Cowey and his tommy gunners searched for more Australians. Then Cowey led them to Deniki, collecting a few more stragglers along the way. Once the sun was up, the Australians worked their way up the hill beside the airstrip, and then watched in disbelief as two Allied Kittyhawk fighter-bombers flew almost level with them, dropping ammunition and other supplies to the Japanese soldiers who now had control of the airstrip.

At one point, Cowey stopped the group when he saw twigs and leaves floating down a creek. The bushman realised that there was somebody in the creek, further up. Circling, he spotted a Japanese patrol post and, setting up a machine gun, Cowey calmly shot the gunner. When another soldier rolled in to fire the gun, Cowey shot him, and another, but as the Japanese party was larger, and the Australians' ammunition was running low, they withdrew, and returned to the main force at Deniki.

Jim Cowey

Jim Cowey, was a World War I veteran who had joined the AIF as a private in 1914. He rose from the ranks to be a lieutenant and acting company commander in the infantry by the end of that war. He must have been a fierce warrior as he was mentioned in dispatches and awarded the Military Cross for a second exploit. Cowey was wounded twice, one a serious head wound, but he fought on to the end of World War I.

An expert bushman and a crack shot, Cowey saw the inevitable approach of World War II and joined the militia as an infantry instructor. His training may explain why the 39th Battalion performed so well in battle. Cowey survived all of the battles fought by the 39th and he was discharged as a private, late in 1943. It remains a mystery that a man who added so much to the survival of the 39th men received so little recognition, either then or since. Under normal circumstances, a decorated hero like Cowey would have been made an officer in the militia, but it did not happen.

There is a hidden story here, about the soldier Jim Cowey. Before the war began in Europe, Germany invaded Czechoslovakia while the rest of the world stood and watched. It was too much for Jim Cowey, who packed up his World War I medals and sent them back to the Australian government. It was a gesture of contempt from a hero who had fought 'the war to end all wars', a war he had fought to make the world a safer place. The return of his medals was a public show of disgust.

Jim Cowey had spent part of the first war teaching young men how to stay alive. In World War II he taught another generation and then stood guard over them to ensure their safety.

Cowey was utterly loyal to his commanders and his troops, but he was also fiercely outspoken when an officer made an incompetent decision — he was a political radical.

Perhaps it was his previous behaviour in returning his medals or his outspoken attitude that resulted in the lack of recognition he received by the end of the war. Maybe it was both.

Days 20 to 30 Deniki

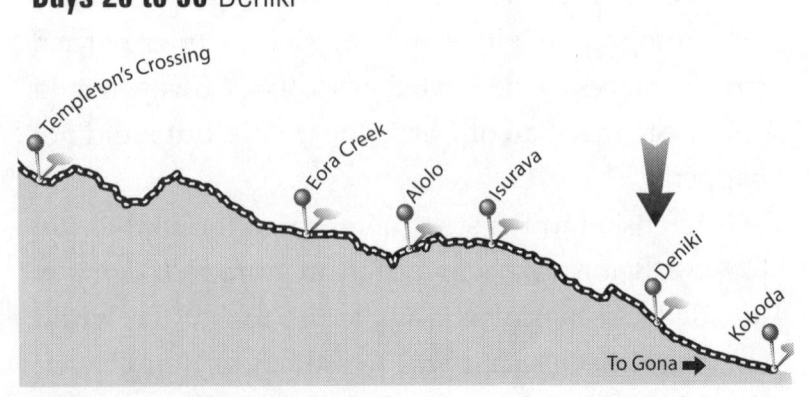

The men on the ground, the ones who survived, were learning fast. On day 20, 13 August, the Japanese had moved out of Kokoda and were aiming to take the village of Deniki. Lieutenant Simonson's platoon from the 39th Battalion fought off a Japanese attack with grenades and tommy guns. Later, Simonson, a clerk in civilian life, heard mess tins rattling. He crept forward, spotting Japanese soldiers at lunch. He left, but not before knocking out two machine guns and a number of men with grenades. That effort earned him the Military Cross, a high award for bravery.

On day 21, some Australian troops were cut off and Cameron ordered a withdrawal. The cut-off troops would later rejoin the battalion. Incredibly, with Japanese troops already at Deniki (beyond Kokoda, an easy 3-hour march, but at the start of the hard climb), Thomas Blamey still advised the government that the Japanese were unlikely to mount an overland attack.

On Day 22, Brigadier Arnold Potts of the 21st Brigade, AIF arrived at Myola with expectations of fresh supplies to relieve the 39th. But there had been no supply drop since 16 August and the small force at Myola had not been advised of Potts's impending arrival. There were only five days' supplies instead of the promised 25. When this news was relayed to Port Moresby, a consignment of supplies was dropped at Myola between 23 and 24 August. The drop included green uniforms.

Only around 30 per cent of the drop survived intact.

Blamey may have been advising that a Japanese overland attack was unlikely, but by 22 August,

Major General Arthur Samuel 'Tubby' Allen

Arthur Allen was born in Hurstville, Sydney. He was an audit clerk with the railways until he joined the cadets, then the AIF in 1915. In 1940 he served in the Middle East. He was given command of the 7th Division — which included the 21st and 25th Brigades — against the Vichy French in Syria and he was promoted to general in March 1942. In August 1942 he took charge against the Japanese advance on Port Moresby.

around 6000 Japanese combat troops had landed at Gona or were advancing toward Kokoda. Each soldier carried 15 days worth of rations as well as equipment in his pack.

On day 31, 24 August, Brigadier Arnold Potts took charge of Maroubra Force. Potts was a highly-decorated soldier. He had earned the Military Cross and been mentioned in dispatches in World War I, when he rose to captain. In Syria, he added a Distinguished Service Order and was again mentioned in dispatches.

It was perfectly clear to Potts that the enemy were headed for Port Moresby and that somehow he and his Maroubra Force would have to stop them, roll them back, and defeat them. That would mean a lot of serious rethinking, starting with the soldiers' uniforms.

Brigadier Arnold William Potts

Arnold William Potts was a grazier who joined the AIF in 1915 after serving in cadets and the Australian Citizens' Military Forces. He became an acting sergeant in the AIF at the age of 18. He was posted to Gallipoli in July 1915, and by 1918, he was a captain in France, with the Military Cross and a chest wound that almost killed him.

In April 1940, at the age of 44, he joined the second AIF as a major and helped establish the newly-formed 2/16th Battalion. This battalion did fine work against the Vichy French in Syria.

He was promoted to lieutenant colonel, given command of the 2/16th Battalion and awarded the Distinguished Service Order (DSO). The 2/16th Battalion was part of one of the three brigades in Tubby Allen's 7th Division.

Potts took command of the 21st Brigade — the first AIF troops to arrive at Port Moresby. The Brigade consisted of the 2/14th Battalion, 2/16th Battalion and 2/27th Battalion.

Imagine a letter to home...

They say the problem with war is that generals are always fighting the one before, all over again. They reckon the plans for the Gallipoli landings were drawn up in 1854, 61 years before they landed at Anzac Cove, and some people reckoned Blamey learned all about soldiering in the mud of Flanders, and thought us soldiers in New Guinea were fighting in trenches dug in open countryside.

Maybe that was part of it, but Blamey never even came to New Guinea until the fighting was almost over. We were there and we certainly didn't know what to expect, so how could he? We knew nothing about camouflage, but those of us who didn't get killed quickly saw how the Japanese did it, and passed the word on.

We solved part of the challenge of operating in the jungle when gradually we learned there were tracks and animal pads that could be followed and stream beds that could be clambered along.

Mastering the jungle also meant learning to keep track of direction when there was no sun to navigate by.

In the Australian bush, people use four main clues to find their way: where the sun or the moon is, distant landmarks, the slope of the land and compass bearings. Most of the time, the first two clues are enough, but in the jungle, you can't see the sun or the moon, or landmarks, so you navigate by knowing which valley you are in and where you are in the valley, and what compass bearing you have been moving on. It took us a while to learn how to do that.

It wasn't just the cold that was depressing — the whole jungle was weird. Coming back down afterwards, we had to go slowly and take lots of breaks. That's when I noticed the ants taking an easy way along the telephone wire that sigs had strung along from tree to tree, beside the track. We had to squeeze around each other or stand back while fresh troops went up, and that was when I figured out how the ants did it. The ants going uphill travelled on top of the wire while those going down used the underside. Clever, that — guess they'll take over the world one day.

On the way up, there was a network of fine roots on the track that gave you something to grip onto. When we came back, though, thousands of military boots had broken the roots away and there was nothing to stop you slipping. I didn't mind, because I was still alive and I wasn't on a stretcher. The only holes in me were some tropical ulcers that could be fixed with zinc ointment and bandages.

Night was a black hole of uncertainty. The Japs liked to attack at night, so we slept with one eye closed and the other open — just in case.

One night we kept hearing movement in the scrub. Some of my mates opened fire on the movement from where they were sleeping in their weapons pits — shallow trenches half-filled with water.

In the morning we found the culprit.

The night before, one of the blokes had washed his singlet and hung it up to dry on a bush. It seems it had been flapping in the breeze all night. The bloke's singlet was now full of bullet holes.

He laughed and said that at least it showed we were good shots.

Chapter 5
Fighting on the Track

The militia had been trained to fight against Japanese coming from the sea, over open ground. They expected to be fighting from prepared defences, and to have artillery backup. Instead, they had found themselves up to their shins in putrid mud, dressed in khaki uniforms that might suit desert warfare but which were hopelessly light-coloured in jungle. They did not know their environment. They did not know how to move in jungle.

The AIF troops who followed the militia were men who had grown tough in the deserts of North Africa against the Germans, and in Syria against the French Foreign Legion.

From 9 March 1942, 20,000 Australian troops arrived at Adelaide and Perth. They were men who knew how to fight in the arid limestone country of the Mediterranean. They were trained in southern Queensland in 'jungle' — training that was later regarded as of no use at all. For their training in Queensland to be effective they should have been in the far north, up on Cape York. In fact, these men, 20,000 of Australia's most qualified soldiers, were used to reinforce the coastline while the militia in Isurava prepared to meet the Japanese advancement.

Many people knew of the track's existence in July 1942, but few understood its physical terrain. The Japanese knew it was there, like the Australian administrators, but it was just a line across the map to them — the actual track was unknown territory. The Allied commanders received warnings about the Japanese using the track to attack Port Moresby two months before the Japanese landed, so why did nobody investigate the conditions on the track?

One theory is that a jungle guerrilla war was not the sort of war that General Douglas MacArthur was interested in fighting. He ignored the threat of invasion over the track and kept planning for sea invasion and attacks by air. General Blamey ignored the threat as well. By early June, though, both generals knew of the Japanese plans. Even then, they gave no orders that challenged those plans.

The track

The first thing the track did from the Sogeri plateau was to plunge downwards, dodging around, through and over rushing streams until it came to a river that could be crossed by a rickety bridge, or that had to be waded through. Then the track launched back up into the sky again.

The combination of heavy rain and volcanic soil meant mud was never far away. There were easier sections now and then, but soldiers paid for these easy bits when they reached another horror climb.

Even going downhill was difficult — when you have a track that is often used, the mud can get deep.

Remember the track was just a faint line that was worn down by bare human feet, and maybe by a few animals.

On an ordinary day, a few people might walk along it, but normally, the track had time to recover. When the track went up a hill, and five hundred soldiers climbed it, all of them wearing boots, and a thousand carriers walked up it one day and back down it the next, passing another thousand going up, there was no time for the water to drain away from deep footprints, and soon the whole track was mud.

The tramp of heavy feet broke down the roots that held everything in place, and the track began to ooze.

Then the engineers had to come along with axes, saws and hammers, to make the track solid again. They would cut down trees and make stairs for the soldiers and carriers to climb, but it was never an easy way to go uphill.

To understand the amount of mud, you have to realise that the area gets five metres of rain a year, and sometimes got 250 mm on a single day. Added to that, the men were not able to step off the track to relieve themselves, so there was not just ordinary mud, but stinking mud.

Throughout the fighting, there was a lot of talk from outsiders about the Kokoda 'pass' or 'gap', which was

The 'Golden Stairs' of the Kokoda Track.

imagined as some sort of narrow chasm that could be easily blocked and held.

In fact the 'gap' was just a lower area of the ridge that was used by aircraft flying from south to north and back again. The gap the pilots used was only about 2000 metres above sea level, but the track itself never went on the lowest part of the ridge.

Even in September, when everybody should have known the conditions, Australian war correspondent, George Johnston noted in his diary that, ' … we have been forced almost completely out of the mountain pass through the Owen Stanleys …'

The existence of this mythical pass was the standard line in public announcements coming from the MacArthur headquarters, along with his private claims to the Australian government that the Australians were not fighting hard enough, and were being defeated by a tiny group of Japanese. People who had been there knew better.

The Golden Stairs
The 'golden stairs' was one of the climbs over Imita Ridge, at the start of the track. Built by army engineers, it was incredibly steep. Soon after the war, Dudley McCarthy wrote, 'From Uberi, the track rose 1200 feet in three miles, dropped 1600 feet, then rose 2000 feet in four miles.' The 'stairs' were 25 to 45 cm in height, each with a log held in place by stakes, and behind each log, a mud puddle.

Each side of the track is steep but not sheer and nowhere does it crawl around a cliff face. There are some very steep pinches, but the general climb is fairly easy.

When you reach the head of the valley the track goes straight over the back of a broad saddle, about 10 kms wide. There's no narrow neck to hold; no position that can't be outflanked.

Wilmot explained the multiple tracks problem, and told anybody who would listen that the flanks were not protected by impenetrable jungle, as most people thought.

But Blamey and MacArthur weren't listening.

What the jungle is like

The war correspondent, Chester Wilmot also told people how rainforest could be quite thick, but not impassable. You could get through it, he said, but it was still thick enough to provide cover. It was thick enough to hide an attacker, but open enough to let attackers push through.

He finished up: 'This means that you needed a large force to hold this saddle and we didn't have a force large enough to counter the outflanking moves the Japanese made.'

Jungle is variable. It may all look the same at first, but when you look more closely you see there are different types of jungle. Even so, some things are constant, like lawyer vine.

The lawyer vine gets its name from the hooks that occur along it. Once you walk into it, people say, it never lets go — just like a lawyer.

On the tops of ridges, where the water drains away, the growth is thinner, and that can sometimes mean there are bushes and vines and shrubs on the ridge, but at other times, it can be clear.

One thing you can be sure of: every creek bed will be a jumble of rocks washed down in a wet season flood, with vines, branches, scrubby trees and dead wood, all tangled in together.

The rocks and the logs offer deadly slippery surfaces, but with time, you learn there is a certain safety in travelling along creeks because the creek bed only goes one way, and it will eventually come out on a ridge.

When they first arrived, the Australians could only see jungle, but as time went on, they learned how to tell one sort from another, and how to choose the best sort of jungle to travel through.

The Jungle Deep
Chester Wilmot told his radio listeners: 'It's so thick that if you get 100 yards off the track you'd easily get lost. One officer did — he pushed his way through the jungle some 200 yards looking for some stores. When he turned to come back he couldn't find his own tracks. He wandered for nearly two days before he found his way back ... and he was an experienced bushman who had trekked alone through the Kimberleys for years.'

Camouflage

The khaki uniforms of the Australian troops were useless, dangerous even, in the jungle war zone, but General Blamey said there was no problem, even though he had never been near either the fighting, or the New Guinea jungle.

In New Guinea, Chester Wilmot, Osmar White and George Johnston were the best of the best. When Blamey visited New Guinea on 13 September, Chester Wilmot asked him, in a press conference, about the uniforms.

Blamey and Wilmot hated each other, and Blamey's curt replay was that khaki had been designed in India as the best camouflage colour for jungle. He said that he had no evidence that this jungle was any different from the Indian jungle.

Wilmot had been on the track, and he had seen what was going on. He had also talked to ordinary soldiers, NCOs and officers.

Wilmot made his contempt for Blamey plain as he replied that he could refer him to some thousands who thought otherwise.

Some of them were in Blamey's army, because the 25th Brigade of the AIF had arrived in Port Moresby dressed in jungle greens, four days earlier.

Power games are played by odd rules. Wilmot was the worst person to raise the khaki question, because he hated Blamey, and Blamey loathed him.

They had very different political ideas, and it

was widely known that Wilmot was looking for evidence that Blamey had taken bribes or kickbacks in the Middle East.

To Blamey, Wilmot was the enemy, and anything he said was to be ignored.

Even when the Australians were given green clothing, many of them did not wear the new clothes. When they did, their white hands and faces and their khaki webbing and gaiters still showed up against the dark green jungle. It took time to learn jungle warfare. Many soldiers died simply because they had not streaked their hands and faces with mud.

There was more to survival than camouflage, but without that the troops had no chance. In late 1942, when the first American troops were ready to leave for New Guinea, Blamey's headquarters staff advised there was no need to dye their uniforms. General Robert Eichelberger, a fighting soldier who commanded the Americans, ignored the advice and studied film taken of New Guinea by news cameraman Damien Parer. Then Eichelberger discussed conditions on the track with Parer and war correspondent Osmar White, who had both experienced the jungle conditions. Based on the newsmen's advice, Eichelberger decided to dye the US uniforms a mottled green.

War Correspondents

In 1854, the Crimean war saw the introduction of war correspondents. The British army was equipped with a telegraph line that ran all the way back to London, so *The Times* sent a correspondent to report on the war. The only problem was that the *Times* journalist, William Russell, talked to ordinary soldiers and informed his readers of the unpleasant truth about the war — the generals had to learn to manage the correspondents.

Some of Australia's World War II newsmen were among the very best war correspondents ever seen. In New Guinea there was Chester Wilmot, Osmar White and George Johnston.

Chester Wilmot reported not only to his radio listeners but also to the generals, letting them know what he had seen. Damien Parer took film that shaped how all Australians see and understand Kokoda, even today. Osmar White and Chester Wilmot were on the scene early, and carefully self-censored their work, as well as having the army censors check their comments in case they gave away any secrets.

There was one point where a newspaper in Chicago let slip that the Allies were reading coded Japanese signals, but, luckily, word of this never got out to the Japanese.

If it had, the war could have taken a very different turn.

Herald *war correspondent, Osmar White, and Chester Wilmot of the ABC at their camp on the Kokoda front.*

Censorship was used to keep the army's secrets from the enemy, but it was also used to shape the information that the Allies received. MacArthur's staff used censorship to present their general as a hero. The Australian journalist George Johnston passed on this standard line when he was with MacArthur's staff, but when he published his diaries later, they show that he quickly realised he was being used.

The correspondents presented a good picture of what the troops were doing. They had walked alongside the telephone lines that ran from headquarters, all the way to the front lines, they knew how isolated commanders were from the realities of the fighting, and they were committed to carrying that story back.

The intelligent commanders, like Syd Rowell, paid attention to what they were told. Thomas Blamey, on the other hand, was not happy with the information he was receiving and set out to ignore and bury any reports that came back from the correspondents that did not meet with his approval.

Imagine reading the diary of a Japanese soldier...

I cannot find Akio and suspect that he is either lost or dead.

Each night I fear that I will not wake to see another day. It is dark in the jungle, a darkness that goes beyond anything I have known before. The night is not quiet here. There are sounds that I cannot identify. The rustling of a branch can be an animal, a friend or foe. I have stopped fearing every noise. I sometimes think it would be easier to bring glory to my family and die for my country.

I cannot decide which event I would wish for Akio.

The canopy of trees above is dense. I have not seen the sky for days. Sometimes I feel I will suffocate with the closeness of this jungle. Yet I know it is this very terrain that helps to conceal me.

Each day I pray to the morning sun that filters through from above. I pray that soon the Imperial Army will celebrate a victorious arrival in Port Moresby.

Each night I pray that this will all come to an end.

Our officers are forever urging us to be patient. So we wait. Our tactics are to encircle and surprise. When the enemy is in sight we fire. We must not miss. The enemy cannot be allowed to escape. Sometimes I find it hard to keep a steady hand.

My thoughts are constantly about food. It seems we

have fewer rations each day, but the officers are still looking robust and well-fed. It is not for me to question the right or wrong of this situation. I add to my rice ration with whatever food this inhospitable land provides me. Today it was snake.

Rain is a constant reminder that I am not in my homeland. It soaks through my uniform, through my skin and into my bones. My body suffers the fevers of malaria and sends me into unsettled sleep. In my dreams I am dry and well fed and safe in the arms of my family.

It is only upon waking that my nightmares begin.

Chapter 6
Tactics

Chester Wilmot wrote about the Japanese camouflage in some detail: 'The Japs have developed the camouflage of their troops to a very high degree. Near Kokoda they've been wearing deep, close-fitting steel helmets with green veils that cover their faces. They wear sweaters and trousers of mottled green and the net result is that they are very hard to see. They are trained to stand still beside a tree trunk for long periods waiting for a chance to strike.'

Some Australian soldiers dyed their own uniforms green but most troops were still wearing light khaki which afforded no protection in the mottled green jungle of the Kokoda Track.

An official historian, Dudley McCarthy, likened the Japanese methods to those of South American soldier ants. He explained that they were trained and experienced in jungle warfare, they lived on simple foods and they were not tied to their supply lines.

What he chose not to mention (or did not know) was that some Japanese soldiers had resorted to cannibalism — eating dead Australian and Japanese soldiers — to keep from starving. The evidence of this was found on bodies, in abandoned camps, and also in at least one captured diary. But the Japanese were not alone in this. The historian, Paul Ham, has suggested that some Australian soldiers, lost in the jungle and starving for weeks, ate one of their own dead to stay alive. For those who endured the starvation of the jungle, this came to be an understandable, albeit truly horrific, act.

The Japanese soldiers used the ground well, trying to get to the high ground with their mountain guns and mortars. They also used English speakers to try to confuse the issue, but it generally did not work.

On one occasion, Australians heard a voice in the jungle calling, 'Don't shoot, it's Ernest'. They opened fire, arguing that no Australian would call himself 'Ernest'. He would be Ernie or have a nickname of some sort.

They also tried calling orders in English, but the Australians had an answer for that, as correspondent George Johnston noted in his diary: 'AIF units who've been two and a half years in the Middle East got around the Japanese using English by their platoon commanders giving orders in Arabic.'

When a major attack was about to start on day 17, as A Company held the airstrip at Kokoda, the Japanese soldiers began a fierce chant, designed to frighten the enemy. Then an English-speaking Japanese officer called out, asking the Australians if it had frightened them. The Australians jeered back — probably a mistake, because it indicated to the Japanese where the Australians were.

Australian tactics and equipment

The Australians' best tactic was their ability to hit and fade away, only to hit again. To ambush, withdraw and ambush again; to hold the ground while others, further up the track, prepared a new defence, to wear the enemy down, to make sure that every small gain by the enemy was a hard slog.

They did not have enough ammunition or weapons. They did not have the numbers to fight a pitched battle. Still, General Morris in Port Moresby had promised reinforcements if the airstrip could be taken again, and they still believed that the aim of the fight was to keep the airstrip out of Japanese hands.

Slowly, as the rest of the 39th Battalion arrived over the track, the young men who survived became hardened soldiers. They learned to move quietly and live. They learned the battle tactics of the Japanese and how to deal with them. Each attack involved a frontal assault where Japanese troops were sacrificed in

Passwords

Film stars' names were always very popular as passwords, mainly because they were so well known and easy to recognise... Stumbling back through the darkness one night an Australian soldier was suddenly challenged, 'Hayworth?'
'Howgarth' answered the wanderer.
Again came the challenge, 'Hayworth?'
'No! Howgarth!'
'Halt! Hayworth?'
'Crikey...what's wrong with you, mate? I've been halted for the last two minutes. And my blasted name's Howgarth!'
— Soldier NX113826, *Stand Easy*, published for The Australian Military Forces by Australian War Memorial, Canberra ACT, 1945.

Jungle Travel
The slopes, going up and coming down, were the worst part. Osmar White, a war correspondent, wrote: 'You need four times the energy to carry a 50-pound pack up and down razorbacks, compared with ordinary climbing with no pack. The engineers had been improving the track: one section of clay had taken some of the men of the 39th 17 hours to travel 600 yards...'
When the Japanese landed in Gona in July 1942, each soldier carried 100 pounds (approx 45kg) in his pack. Inside the pack were provisions for two weeks, including rice, a first aid kit and weapons.

large numbers, but at the same time, other Japanese soldiers would try to outflank the Australian positions.

The Japanese knew they faced just a small group of men. If they could continue surrounding small groups and wiping them out, soon there would be no opposition left. So the Japanese outflankers tried to get onto the track behind the defenders, to stop reinforcements moving up while they attacked the defenders from behind.

This was where earlier jungle training paid off for the Japanese. Initially the Australians thought of the jungle away from the track as a no-go area, but the Japanese knew there were ways through. The Japanese knew how to find the faint tracks of animals or streams, or how to move onto the next ridge to swing around wide and back onto the track again.

Soon the Australian soldiers also understood this, and they became tougher, more able to work up and down the slopes, to find their way, to read the signs as Jim Cowey did.

Troops learned to be quiet. Lieutenant Simonson's grenade attack on the lunching Japanese highlighted that. War correspondent Osmar White told later how he went out one night with a patrol of newly-arrived soldiers — raw troops who were noisy and clumsy. White stayed with them until just before sunrise, but he was frightened the whole time that they would draw fire upon themselves.

The big challenge was the way the Japanese worked around a position, outflanking it and cutting it off. The Australians found that the Japanese would usually cut the telephone wire. When something like that warned them, the Australians began to slip off the track themselves, outflanking the outflankers, and joining up again with the main force.

When they could, they countered the outflanking method by giving ground slowly, making the invaders pay for each yard they gained. This was no retreat, but a fighting withdrawal that drew the Japanese on, wearing them down, saving lives on the Australian side, but preventing a rapid advance of the Japanese over the Owen Stanley Range and down onto Port Moresby.

Slowly, the Japanese supply lines grew longer as they pushed the Australians up the track, back towards Port Moresby. This transferred the Australians' supply problem to the enemy, who now had to carry their supplies further than the Australians. As the Australians lost ground, extra Australian troops were gradually being brought in and made ready. The longer the 39th Battalion held the enemy up, the easier it would be to stop them and roll them back.

Back in Australia, the generals were screaming for a major victory. The militia, the looked-down-on chockos, had seen far more real fighting than the generals, and they went about doing things their way. 'Death or glory' sounds fine from a distance, but the generals wanted the soldiers' deaths and the generals' glory and, somehow, the soldiers didn't like that idea much.

They wanted to be cunning.

And they were, gloriously so.

Imagine the Battle of Thermopylae, 480BC...

Thermopylae, yes, I remember the men who fought there. We all do. It was drummed into us as boys, but I never let on that I was there when it happened.

The Persians had taken my goats and I was hiding. I was on a hill near the fighting and watched the battle unfold before me. When it was all over, I ran away. You must understand, I was only a young boy — too young to fight.

The battle was very uneven. The Persians had a huge army and there were just a few thousand Greeks. The Persian army was so huge it was like a horde of locusts and they had to keep on the move, just to find food. That was why they took my goats, I suppose.

There was a pass at Thermopylae near my goat mountain, just wide enough for three men to walk through side-by-side, between cliffs and mountains, with a wall to defend and this giant Persian army to keep out.

They say Xerxes, the Persian, could not believe the Greeks would fight, so he let them know he was there and waited four days for them to run. This was a bad decision by Xerxes. He obviously did not know that Greeks do not run away. Then Xerxes sent in the Medes, tough troops and the Greeks yelled and ran away. Then the Medes cheered and broke ranks to chase the Greeks down. This was another bad decision. As I have said, Greeks do not run away.

Once the Medes were disorganised, the Greeks stopped yelling and running away. They turned and butchered the Medes.

Xerxes then sent in his Immortals — his toughest troops. They were tough, but also slow to learn. When the Greeks yelled and ran away, the Immortals followed them. They too were turned upon and butchered.

Later I learned of a Greek, a man called Ephialtes, who went to Xerxes and told him about another path that could be used to get through the mountains. The Persians used the path to outflank our army, to get behind the Greeks.

When our leader Leonidas realised he had been outflanked, and the Immortals would attack him from behind, he dismissed the Greek army, all except 300 Spartans, and 700 Thespians and Thebans. They fought the Persians to a standstill until the Persians had the idea of standing off and hitting the Greeks with arrows and spears. They wiped our heroes out.

Then the Persians moved on, but the main part of the Greek army had got away to fight again and warn the Athenians. The Persians burned Athens, but not the Athenians, who had time to flee.

In the end, the Persians went home and never came back. Without the Greek warriors who held the Persians up at Thermopylae, the Persians would probably have won the war against us.

Good, strong Greeks were killed at Thermopylae.
They died fighting.
They died so that many others would live to fight another day.

Chapter 7
Australia's Thermopylae

Isurava

Isurava is a village on one of the tracks that wind through the landscape south of Kokoda. The phrase 'one of the tracks' is the key to the problem that the Australians faced. There was more than one route through this part of the Range, but back in Australia, Generals Blamey and MacArthur had no maps that showed this. They thought there was just one track, and they knew their history — the generals knew all about Thermopylae.

They knew that the heroic Greeks managed to hold back a much larger Persian army. Still, they insisted that the Australians outnumbered the Japanese, even though all the decoded signals said otherwise.

In one way Isurava was like Thermopylae and yet it wasn't. The 39th Battalion delayed the Japanese long enough for Australian reinforcements to reach Isurava, and then they and the reinforcements held on, withdrawing only when it was essential. But there was no place to make a stand, and the soldiers and officers at Isurava knew it. The delay tactics of Thermopylae were applicable, but that was where the similarities ended. The defenders could not afford to let themselves be wiped out. To fight, withdraw and fight again was a smarter tactic to employ. Isurava was like Thermopylae because it was a brilliant victory pulled off by a smaller force, but it was different because the aims were different, the lay of the land was completely different, and the result was achieved without the winners needing to die.

Before Isurava

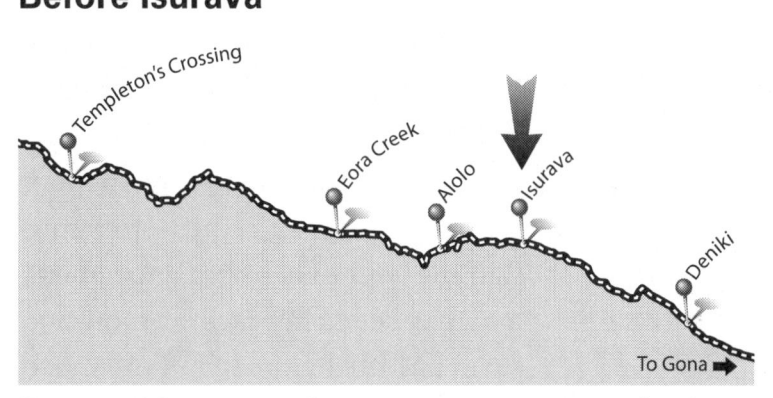

Even without reinforcements, support, food or ammunition, even after the pointless attack at Kokoda airstrip, the fighting spirit of the 39th Battalion was still strong. The troops of the 39th were now six weeks out from Port Moresby. Their clothes and boots were rotting and they lived on a diet of tinned beef and biscuits, yet morale was still high. Now there was help on the way for the 39th. All they had to do was hold on, to slow the Japanese down, to wear them out a bit more.

On 16 August, ten days before the start of the battle at Isurava, the first members of the 53rd Battalion arrived. With them came an experienced AIF officer,

Lieutenant Colonel Ralph Honner

Honner was born in Fremantle, Western Australia. He enlisted in the AIF in October 1939 and fought in the Middle East in 1940. Honner returned to Australia in 1942 and was promoted to Lieutenant Colonel. He was then sent to Port Moresby to take command of the 39th Battalion who were fighting Japanese troops on the Kokoda Track. Honner employed the fighting withdrawal and was awarded the Distinguished Service Order for his leadership and skill as a combat commander.

Lieutenant Colonel Ralph Honner who was appointed to command the 39th Battalion. While Honner had not led troops in jungle conditions, he brought battle skills that would apply anywhere. The 39th now had jungle experience but the troops were frazzled and tired. Honner later wrote of what he saw when he arrived to take command: 'Physically, the pathetically young warriors of the 39th were in poor shape. Worn out by strenuous fighting and exhausting movement, and weakened by lack of food and sleep and shelter, many of them had literally come to a standstill.'

At every point in the long battle the Japanese had many more troops than the Australians, but they never used them all at once. If General Horii had used his troops in an 'all out' attack, he would have broken through. Instead he proceeded cautiously. Rather than employ his numbers to swamp the Australians, Horii used his troops to try to wear the Australians down. The Japanese commander was able to switch battalions between attacking and resting, giving the Japanese soldiers time to regain their strength.

There was very little rest for the Australians, but after they had walked over the Kokoda Track, troops needed some time to recover their strength. The B Company of the 53rd Battalion arrived with Honner, and C Company arrived a day later. Honner sent B Company out on patrol right away, but decided to keep C Company as a reserve, because the troops were worn out after their walk. Looking back, this may have been a mistake, as it stopped the 53rd getting some of the jungle experience they badly needed.

Still, if Honner had made a small error, General Horii made a huge mistake when he waited to build a larger force.

Horii's mistake is understandable. Horii had no idea of what lay in front of him, or what was on the way. The militia had fought far more effectively than such a small force should have done, so he could reasonably have assumed there were many more soldiers waiting up the track than there really were.

General Horii did not know that battle-hardened troops of the AIF had left Australia in early August, and were finally moving up to the front line. There were only three battalions of them, because other AIF troops would be needed to fight off another Japanese landing. Decoded signals revealed that there would be an attack by the Japanese at Milne Bay on the eastern tip of Papua, and that also had to be stopped. Still, there were some experienced fighters coming, and when they arrived the Australian army on the Kokoda Track would become much stronger.

A problem for the Australians was faulty intelligence from those at GHQ in Brisbane to those in charge at Port Moresby. In early August, MacArthur's staff told Brigadier Potts that only 4000 Japanese were on the track, rather than the 6000 who were really there.

Because of a shortage of supplies, Potts was only able to send AIF companies forward when there were enough supplies available for them. One company left Myola on 25 August, at least three days later than scheduled.

That could have had fatal consequences for the 39th Battalion, but the luck of the Australians held.

Myola and the air drops

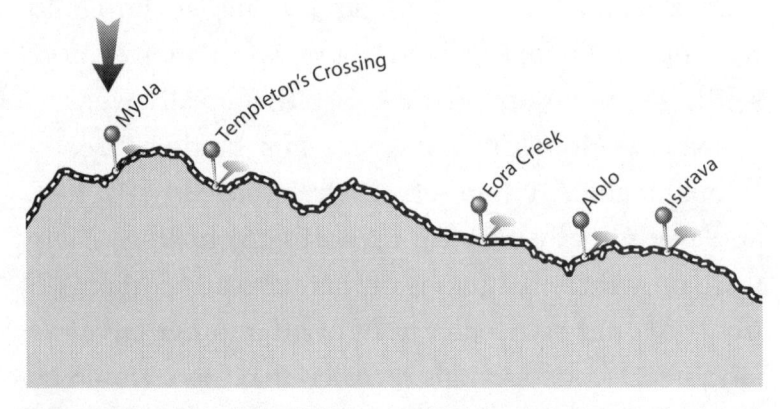

The real struggle of the Kokoda Track was about getting supplies in and the wounded out. A dried lake-bed near Myola, at an altitude of about 2000 metres, not far from Isurava had provided the perfect answer to this problem. Chester Wilmot flew to Myola once, and he said later that it took 35 minutes in a plane to reach a place that took five hard days on foot. This showed how much more effective airdrops could be, even if some of the material was lost.

Lieutenant Bert Kienzle remembered seeing a clear area once when he was in a plane en route from Port Moresby to Kokoda. He decided it might have been one or more dry lake-beds, and went looking for it, or them. After several days, he found two lake-beds covered in long kunai grass, with a creek running through. The area had no local name, so Kienzle gave it what he said later was an Australian Aboriginal name of Myola. As August progressed and the fighting got closer, Myola became a strategic location.

As General Horii massed his troops to attack Isurava, a huge Japanese air raid bombed the Port Moresby Seven-mile Strip on 17 August. This was the first air raid for more than a fortnight and everybody was caught out. The bombs destroyed a long line of transports and bombers that were lined up, wingtip to wingtip. In all, 28 aircraft were damaged, and this interfered badly with delivery of supplies to Myola.

The day before the raid, war correspondents had seen the planes lined up and 'undispersed'. They warned commanders that this put the planes at risk. They were told it would be looked into, 'First thing in the morning', but next morning the bombers arrived. It was too late to move the planes.

Afterwards bomb bays were built at the airfield. These were U-shaped earth piles, higher than a plane and facing different directions, each large enough to hold one plane. If a bomb landed where it could damage one plane, it was in the wrong place to hit any of the others.

Rowell signalled the Australian command for more planes. He told them the procedure for getting transport planes was too slow and had already cost Australia the possession of Kokoda. His clear message was that the troops were using 10 tons of materials and supplies, every day. In Australia, authorities did not seem to understand that to build up a stockpile, more than the daily needs had to be carried each day.

Aside from what was needed every day, there were some days when the weather closed in, so there could be no drops. Besides, not all the dropped stores would land in one piece and be recovered. The troops needed enough planes to deliver 20 tons of supplies on a good day. In the end, General MacArthur approved enough planes to carry just 10 tons a day. Then he told them that air supply had to be regarded as an emergency method, rather than the normal mode of operations. He demanded that the local command in New Guinea develop 'other means of supply'.

Many of the bags dropped out of sight, or the contents were destroyed. Even if they landed safely at Myola, supplies would still have to be carried two or three days to the front. Soon, though, this distance shortened, and later Myola was lost as the Australians continued to fall back under the Japanese attack. Once the Japanese army passed Myola, everything had to be carried in from the head of the track.

Air-drop recoveries were sometimes as high as 80 per cent, but some recoveries fell as low as 10 per cent. When tinned meat was dropped in corn sacks, about 20 per cent of the tins burst on impact. Over time, better systems of marking the drop zones improved recovery, but the main challenge was in getting the right height. The 'biscuit bombers', as the DC3 aircraft were called, needed to come in at a bit over 100 metres. Lower down, the packages might be falling slower, but their forward movement was too great, and the packets smashed. Higher up, the forward movement slowed more, but the downward fall was too great, and they smashed. According to the official versions,

Supply Drops

'The trip proved to be as John had predicted, "just a matter of walking". Mile after mile, ever upward and always winding we trudged along the narrow, boggy track. Two days of this...we came over a crest... Seven (planes) zoomed in circles as low as they dared, and out were thrown grenades, food and bales of blankets... Cases of meat and tins of biscuits hurtled into the swamps or broke upon the hillsides and scattered the contents...Late into the night we were retrieving those precious goods.'
— Soldier NG2057', *Khaki and Green*, published for The Australian Military Forces by Australian War Memorial Canberra, ACT, 1943.

the 'pusher-outers' on the planes were equipped with a safety harness, but the war correspondents who flew and did some of the pushing-out reported they only had a rope tied around their waists and attached to a ringbolt on the plane. A pile of supplies would be set up by the open door, heaviest items on the bottom, and the stacks were pushed on the pilot's signal. The plane flew on a slant, with the door-side wing lower than the other, to make pushing easier, but also making it easier to fall out.

Being a pusher-outer was no fun, but the worst job was on the ground, as 'marker'. The poor marker had to stand close to the dropping area and take compass bearings on loads that fell short or overshot the drop zone, and duck when a drop came too close.

The big problem with air-drops was that ammunition could be damaged. Each round, especially those going into an automatic weapon, had to be checked for damage that might make it jam in the gun. On one occasion, after the troops were issued with mortars, eight of 27 air-dropped mortar rounds that were used in battle failed to explode, while others exploded prematurely, killing the mortar men. Later, hard-to-obtain supply parachutes were used to drop mortar rounds and fuses more gently. Supply parachutes were also used later for machine gun ammunition.

Imagine you are an AIF soldier...

When they bought us back from fighting at Syria, I was just glad to be home on Australian soil. My mate Cliffy kissed the ground when we got off the ship and he got kicked in the bum for it, but we all had a laugh.

After a bit, we were pretty keen to take on those Japs, but the powers-that-be moved us to Queensland and we spent a lot of time mucking around — a bit of building and some jungle training.

Jungle! That's a laugh.

We finally got to Port Moresby and it was different from Syria — and Queensland, if you want to know. We hung around again as we waited for supplies — I don't know who was in charge, but it seemed a shemozzle if you ask me. Then they told us we were off up the track to relieve the 39th Battalion.

'Let's show these chockos how to win a war,' said Cliffy and we all agreed with him.

We walked through the mud and jungle for seven days and joked about how the beardless boys in the militia must have had porters to carry them.

We'd been fighting in Syria, so we reckoned we knew all about it. Professional soldiers, we were. Properly trained, disciplined, crack shots — I guess you could say we had tickets on ourselves.

Anyhow one of the New Guinea hands, an old bloke, was coming down the track as we left Port Moresby. He told us the militia boys were just managing to hold the Japs. We talked it over that night and figured the Japs weren't much chop.

We figured wrong.

We learned that the Japanese troops were like us — professional, tough and disciplined. We realised pretty soon that the militia and the Japs were evenly matched, but it wasn't because the Japs were as weak as the militia, it was because the militia were as strong as the Japanese army.

We finally came into the line (if you could call it a line — it was so ragged) and found the shot-up remnants of the 39th Battalion just holding the Japs at bay.

Our poor buggers barely looked human, but one managed a grin and said, 'About time you blokes got here.'

We learned pretty fast to shut up and listen to those men who'd kept the Japs from Port Moresby. We learned about camouflage, the patience of the snipers and much more besides.

I nearly lost my noggin on the second day when I stood up behind a rock that hid me from the ground in front. One of the 39th pulled my feet from under me, just as a Jap sniper up a tree fired at me.

Well, who would've thought it? There I was, one of the heroes of the AIF, 'Australia's Great Hope', and I was saved from a Jap sniper by a chocko!

Sadly, Cliffy didn't learn as quickly as me. He didn't last the week.

Chapter 8
The Fight for Isurava

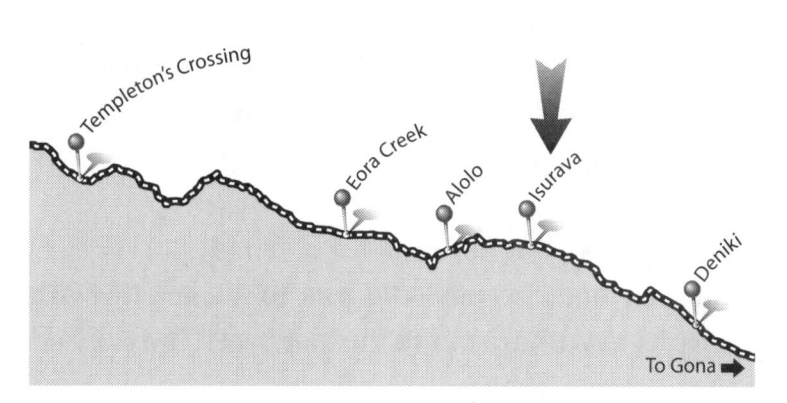

Day 33, 26 August The AIF arrive at Isurava

If General Horii had attacked immediately, he probably would have broken through and so been able to attack the AIF troops while they were still trying to get into the mountains. Time was running out for Horii, who needed to move fast, to reach Port Moresby and take it, but he froze, and that hesitation lost him the fight for New Guinea. He spent 12 days, from 14 to 25 August, assembling 6000 men between Kokoda and Isurava. Then on 26 August, day 33, he moved his troops forward, but he had waited too long.

By then, the first of the AIF troops, C Company of the 2/14th Battalion, were fully equipped, and they had been sent on their way. By now, the militia knew from telephone messages that help was coming. That improved morale, and so did Honner's treatment of the 39th's B Company. Major Cameron had treated B Company as a disgraced unit, but Honner put them in the most challenging position for the coming attack. He gave them the chance to show what they could do, and they rose to the occasion.

Isurava was a good delaying position for Australia. There was cleared ground each side of the track, meaning the Japanese would be exposed as they attacked.

It was good, but not ideal for defence.

Honner had the men dig pits to shelter in, with more pits to withdraw into, further back. The site had heavy jungle to the north and south.

Honner realised the Japanese would mass in scrub to the west with open ground in front, and this is where he placed B Company, displaying his trust in them.

It would be an unequal fight with the Australians outnumbered about four to one, but the Australians would hold up the Japanese advance once again.

The attack began with artillery fire from one of the Japanese mountain guns. These were small guns that could be taken apart and carried to a position where they could be used to drop explosive shells on the defenders. The mountain gun had a much greater range than anything else in the battle, so the guns could sit in perfect safety, dropping shells wherever the crew wanted to put them. The Australians had no way of hitting back.

The only drawback for the mountain gun was that in the jungle it was hard to see where the shells landed, or what they hit, so a lot of the shots were wasted. The Japanese heavy machine guns were used from closer in to shred the flimsy defences, but even those had to be very close if they were to do much damage, and that meant the machine-gunners could be shot with rifles — if they could be seen.

This was where the Japanese camouflage helped most, but attackers need to move, to approach defenders who are keeping still, and human eyes are very good at seeing movement.

This gave the Australian defenders an advantage. The defenders also had luck on their side. Lieutenant Simonson, the grenade enthusiast, was hit by a shot which struck a grenade in his pocket and set off the detonator charge.

He was burned, and his flesh was peppered by bits of the detonator, but the main charge failed to explode, and so he survived.

During the day and the evening of August 26, three companies of the 2/14th Battalion arrived. Things were suddenly looking up for the 39th on day 33, and not before time!

When the AIF soldiers arrived, the taunts of 'chocko soldiers' and 'koalas' were silenced forever.

The new arrivals were stunned by the appearance of the militia, whose clothes were tattered and bodies gaunt.

Day 34, 27 August The failure of one company of the 53rd

So much of the story of Kokoda is the story of incredible heroism and courage and some might think it dishonourable to include an account of the failure of one company of the 53rd Battalion. But an account of this company's failure only highlights how ordinary Australians might have reacted in this jungle war zone. It also highlights a distinct difference between the leadership of the 39th and 53rd Battalions.

The 53rd were poorly led, poorly trained soldiers and they lacked jungle experience. In the heat of battle, some of them began to panic and run. When soldiers run from a fight, it triggers panic among those who remain. Military training teaches you how to fight, but it also teaches you not to run, because it puts you at risk. It happened to other units at other times, but little was said about it.

On occasion, a few of the men of the 39th ran. It happens in every army, and usually it is the people who run who pay the price. While the 39th were holding the main track, the Japanese had managed to get control of part of the eastern track on 25 August. Brigadier Potts ordered the 53rd to move forward, to take back the village of Missima and hold the line so that the defenders at Isurava would not be cut off by a Japanese attack that came up the eastern track and around behind them.

The eastern track plunged 300 metres down

a 45 degree slope, crossed a slippery log bridge and then climbed a slope that could only be tackled if you used both hands and feet. It would be bad enough in peace time, but when you knew there could be a machine-gun-nest waiting to target you, it would have been terrifying.

That is what the 53rd were thrown into, even though Brigadier Potts had already looked them over, and advised headquarters that their discipline and training were 'below standard required for action'.

But Potts had no choice and neither did the 53rd. There could be no support for them, and there was no choice but to use them, because there were no other troops. The 200 soldiers advanced along the track, but then panic broke out. Somebody shouted, 'The Japs have broken through', and company fled into the jungle. Some stayed and their bodies were found later.

Some of the battalion made it back along the track to their camp, and about 70 straggled in over the next few days, after working their

What Really Happened

'We prayed and ran like hell...We had, like many others, escaped the Japs, but were vilified. We were part of that mob. We were blamed for everything...The 53rd had been sent back to Moresby in disgrace. We did not know why. For 60 years I have been trying to find out.'
— Neil Robinson, excerpt from the *Sydney Morning Herald*

way around through the jungle. But is it fair to say that the 53rd failed? Or would it be fairer to say that the commanders failed them, sending untrained men to fight in a savage war? How far up the line do you place the blame?

On day 44, 6 September, Ralph Honner spoke to the men of the 39th. By then the survivors were at Menari, being rested. He reminded them to show some compassion for their fellow comrades. No record exists of what he said, just the recollections of Jack Sim, who was there: 'I can't remember his exact words; but I'll always remember what he meant when he said: "You're all Australians. Some of the men that were with you, you feel have let you down. But they didn't. Given different circumstances, they'd be just the same as you."' That, however, was in the future.

Days 34 to 36 Isurava

On 27 and 28 August, the Japanese soldiers attacked again and again. When we look at a story like this, it is easy to forget that the 'enemy' were also human. The Australian soldiers recognised that they were up against a determined enemy, and they respected this, but they had their orders, and were equally determined. My story is the story of an Australian victory but if we can recognise the bravery of the defeated Anzacs at Gallipoli, we should also try to understand that the Japanese soldiers were equally brave.

Once the desert-trained soldiers of the AIF arrived in PNG they found themselves in a new kind of war. It took them a little while to settle in, but they did so with enough force to make the enemy aware of them. The Japanese reports indicated that there were reinforcements arriving in the Australian lines. Then, on 29 August, a massive attack on the 2/14th Battalion was turned back by the actions of a single man — Bruce Kingsbury — who won the Victoria Cross for his actions.

The Australians had one big advantage, because the attackers had to run up a steep slope. This slowed the Japanese down and made it easier for the defenders. Once the Australians retreated over the hill, they would lose that advantage until they passed the next valley and began to climb again. After that, the fighting would move to the high country, where it would be almost impossible for the Australians to make a stand.

Days 37 to 42, 30 August to 4 September Rolling South

War correspondent, Osmar White reported to his readers in later months how 'General R' (Syd Rowell) had said, early on, 'As far as I'm concerned, I'm willing to pull back and let the enemy have the rough stuff if he wants it... But there are those who think otherwise. We need a victory in the Pacific, and a lot of poor bastards have got to be killed to provide it!'

The big problem was finding a suitable position that could be defended, so the Australians kept pulling back, and this must have raised General Horii's hopes. They pulled back to Eora Creek and held the line there briefly, but on day 40, 2 September, the Australians withdrew again. Now the track split once more, so they had to move south rather fast, and by day 43, they had abandoned the dropping zone at Myola and headed for Efogi, where the tracks joined once more, even though they had been ordered to hold the dropping zone. Before they left, unable to take all the stores with them, Australian troops opened the tins of beef and spilt the sacks of rice on the ground.

The hungry Japanese moved in after the Australians left and feasted on the spoiled meat and rice.

Orders drawn up at Rabaul on 11 August indicated that Horii's forces were to be in Port Moresby by the next full moon, which was on 26 August. Four days after the full moon, the invasion had not yet crossed the Owen Stanley Range. The Japanese supply lines had not yet been strung out, worn out and bombed. The warning signs were there for a wise Japanese general. The vision that Syd Rowell had was coming true.

Private Bruce Steel Kingsbury, VC

At Isurava, on 29 August, the Japanese attacked in such force that they succeeded in breaking through the 2/14th Battalion's right flank, creating serious threats both to the rest of the battalion and to its headquarters. To avoid the situation becoming more desperate, it was essential to regain immediately lost ground on the right flank.

Private Kingsbury engaged in a counter-attack by rushing forward and firing his Bren gun. He kept up a continuous stream of machine-gun fire and succeeded in clearing a path through the enemy. After inflicting a large number of Japanese casualties, Private Kingsbury fell to the ground. He'd been shot dead by a sniper. He was 24 years old.

Private Kingsbury was awarded the Victoria Cross for his actions. It was the first VC gained on territory administered by the Australian Commonwealth.

Corporal John Arthur Metson

One group of the 2/14th Battalion were cut off on day 37, 30 August, with two men on stretchers, three walking wounded and one 'crawling wounded'. This was Corporal Metson, who said that with bandaged pads on his hands and knees he could crawl, freeing the eight or ten men who would otherwise have had to carry him.

Metson had been shot through the ankle, but he refused to be carried. Working their way along Eora Creek, the men moved slowly, led by Captain Ben Buckler, but it was hard going. The party lived by killing isolated Japanese soldiers for their food rations until they shot a pig and had a real feast.

Later, they reached a village called Sengai, hoping to find Australian troops there. Corporal Metson was there with them, still crawling, among them at the last. The villagers fed them and said that the country was rough, and that it would be better to leave the wounded with them.

On day 59, 21 September, the fit men left Metson and the other wounded in the care of Private Tom Fletcher, a medical orderly, and headed off to find help. But help returned too late. A Japanese patrol had reached the village on day 72, 4 October, and killed Metson, Fletcher and the remaining wounded. The wounded were shot on their stretchers and Fletcher was beside them, having stood by his mates to the end.

Imagine you are there...

'There was a lot of talk of men running like rabbits, but you need to ask yourself what you would have done — under the same circumstances. I was there, and I know I was scared. We all were, and it wasn't the first time. Just wait until you're hiding behind a bush and somebody starts shooting at you, and see if you run or not. Bushes aren't bullet-proof!

Anyway, we didn't run. In fact, sometimes the only reason we didn't is that we were too scared to. The Japs had probably come onto the track behind us, because that was their favourite trick. Even if they hadn't, as soon as we ran, they could see us and shoot us, so we knew by then it was safer to stay and fight. So long as nobody else ran, we all stayed and fought, because we had that bit worked out.

Sometimes it made sense to clear out. I was in B Company — the one Cameron called yellow, because we slipped away into the bush. But he was mad. We knew it was pointless to fight and die when we could get away and live to fight another day. I lost one of my uncles at The Nek at Gallipoli when stupid officers sent wave after wave of troops over the top in 1915, and all for nothing. Just a waste of life.

I don't know if I would have gone over the top at The Nek. I guess I would have, because everybody else did, but that was one thing. Hanging around at the Jap-infested Kokoda airstrip was another, so we got out. See, we'd begun to learn, bit by bit, how to fight in the jungle. Some officers talked to us (not Cameron) and what they said made sense. We knew the difference between stupid bravery and common sense. We also knew what fear was, and that's why I don't blame those blokes in the 53rd when they ran, later on.

See, the men in the 53rd were a bit younger than us, not much, and they hadn't had any experience in jungle fighting. They'd just come up into the line with none of the tips we'd picked up on the job. Plus we'd got the best of the officers earlier in the year. Anyhow, I reckon that in their shoes, we'd have run as well. It's just one of those things.

Colonel Honner knew it too, and he said as much later. He was right, too — but that was Honner for you. A genuine bloke.

Chapter 9
General Horii's Plan Falters

Each time there was a skirmish or a fire fight, the Japanese were slowed down some more. Horii's plan was failing, and even he must have seen this by September. The Japanese still had many more troops, they still had far better equipment, but now their supply lines were getting longer. The Allies had control of the skies, so Allied planes could attack Japanese supply lines all the way back to the coast and out to sea.

The Japanese were also using local people as carriers, but they didn't have people such as Doc Vernon or Bert Kienzle to keep the carriers on side. Some Japanese mistreated the New Guinea men. As a result, the carriers often 'went bush', dropping their loads or stealing them.

Each day on the track saw the Japanese using up food and ammunition with no chance of their supplies being replaced. Now the Australians had to keep up the pressure on their enemy. The Japanese were experiencing the supply headaches that Syd Rowell had foreseen long before, but Syd Rowell had been replaced in late September 1942 by Lieutenant General Edmund Herring. Herring had the confidence of Blamey and would not upset his senior officers.

But why did it take so long to get reinforcements onto the Kokoda Track? To understand this, we need to return to May 1942.

Milne Bay

In May, General MacArthur had ordered two bases with airstrips — one at Dobodura on the north coast and the other on the eastern tip of the island at Milne Bay. These were both to be used to attack Rabaul, though Milne Bay would also be a good base from which to attack Japanese shipping. By early July, there was a usable airstrip at Milne Bay, but Japanese reconnaissance planes came back with what looked like evidence that it was not ready for use. They got it wrong.

The decoded signals that showed Japanese plans to land on the northern end of the Kokoda Track also revealed that they planned to attack Milne Bay, and for once, the threat was taken seriously. On 7 July, General Blamey ordered a whole militia brigade, three battalions, to Milne Bay, but sent nothing more to Port Moresby.

When Japanese forces stormed ashore on the night of 25 August, they rushed into a trap of their own making. They were outnumbered. The fighting was fierce, but what had seemed to be easy pickings turned out to be a well-armed and prepared base. The remnants of the Japanese force retreated from Milne Bay on 5 September, day 43 of the Kokoda campaign.

Of the 2400 Japanese troops that stormed Milne Bay, 1147 were either wounded or dead. The Australian troops suffered only 313 of the same.

Now the Allies could afford to move some of the troops from Milne Bay to the Kokoda Track, but more importantly, the 2/27th Battalion, waiting in Port Moresby to be sent wherever the need was greatest, could move up the track. Maroubra Force — as the combination of AIF, militia and PIB troops was known — had been battered, tattered and shredded, and they needed fresh and battle-ready support.

Now it could come.

Day 43, 5 September Over the Range

In the fighting withdrawal over the Owen Stanley Range to Efogi on 5 September, the 39th, 2/14th and 2/16th Battalions were down from 1650 combat troops to less than a third of that. Still they fought every inch of the track, and there were no running rabbits here. Often 20 men would stay, holding off the Japanese, while the rest withdrew and set up a new ambush position. Each metre of track gained by the Japanese was costing them dearly.

There was help at hand in the form of 2/27th AIF Battalion. These soldiers had been held in reserve as other troops fought another desperate battle at Milne Bay. Once the Japanese had been beaten there, the desperately needed 2/27th Battalion was released to head up the Kokoda Track. Soon, other AIF troops would follow them but, for now, the reinforcements were only just keeping up with the losses of dead and wounded men.

Rowell understood what was needed for a military victory, and that was to give the Japanese army supply headaches. Sadly, he had commanders over him who wanted a quick victory at any cost. By this time, Rowell was close to being forced out of his command because he had failed to deal courteously with officials who wanted to tell him what to do, even when they knew nothing of conditions on the track.

The armchair warriors still believed in the mythical 'gap'. A member of MacArthur's staff, General Sutherland, on advice from another American, Major-General Hugh J. Casey, Chief Engineer at GHQ, wrote to Rowell suggesting that '…reconnaissance be made of critical areas on the trail through the Owen Stanley Range for the selection of points where the pass may be readily blocked by demolition, and that the necessary charges be emplaced in the most forward areas and assembled for ready installation in the rear areas.'

Sutherland was proud to call himself MacArthur's SOB — a hatchet-man. He was a politician rather than a soldier, but Syd Rowell was a soldier and he replied to Sutherland with a firm answer: 'The amount of explosive which could be carried by native porters for the five days' trip at present needed to reach the top of the Owen Stanley Range would hardly increase the present difficulties of the track... It is respectfully suggested that such explosives as can be got forward would be better employed in facilitating our advance than for preparing to deny the enemy!'

Rowell's savage reply was his downfall. He should have pointed out more gently that the Range lacked 'critical areas' of the sort imagined by the 'experts' in Brisbane. He should also have reminded the critics of the desperate shortage of basics, like food and ammunition. As it was, MacArthur and his staff continued to carry on about the need to hold the mythical pass. And because they controlled the information passed on to the Australian press, the Australian public and politicians swallowed the MacArthur line.

Rowell had to be dismissed and he would be, just as soon as his commanders could find an excuse.

By now, the 39th Battalion had been taken out of the battle line, and they were getting a break, further up the track at Menari. It was there that Ralph Honner presented his moving speech alluding to the 53rd.

The 39th Battalion's numbers had dropped from 470 to 180, and about a quarter of those were lightly wounded or recovering from sickness or wounds, but they would all be back fighting soon enough.

The 2/14th and 2/16th and 2/27th were still fighting and, on day 45, they saw a pleasing sight. They had been forced out of Efogi onto higher ground and, during the night, they watched the lights as

Japanese soldiers streamed into Efogi, using lengths of Australian telephone wire to hold up flaming torches that lit the way. The Japanese were too far away to hit, and the Australians wished they had mountain guns, like the Japanese. Arnold Potts made a phone call. The next morning, 12 Allied planes bombed and strafed the Japanese forces while the Australians cheered.

Down in the valley, many of the Japanese who survived were suffering dysentery from eating the spoiled rations the Australians had left behind at Myola. The Australians would not know it for a while, but the Japanese war machine was running out of fuel.

Day 44 to 46, 6 to 8 September Butcher's Hill

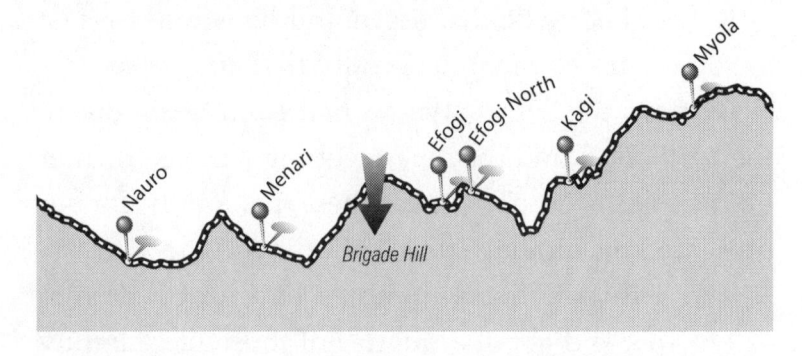

Some of the most savage fighting happened at a location that is known by three names. Some call it Mission Ridge, because of the old mission building there. The official name was Brigade Hill, but the soldiers called it by a more descriptive name — Butcher's Hill. The Japanese attack was so strong here that at one point a number of them approached the Brigade HQ.

Now while the people there were in uniform and had rifles, they were not really fighting men. They were the runners, signalmen, cooks, clerks and storemen — people who were essential to the brigade running smoothly. Their job was to support the fighters. Aged from 35 to 45, they were fit enough to walk in over the track, but that was about it. At Brigade Hill, the Toothless and the Ruthless, as they were affectionately known, proved to be just that, grabbing their weapons and forcing the attackers away again.

It was the same old story: fight, hold the line while new defences are dug, and slip away to fight again from the new defences. Slog through the mud, sleep in the mud, wear the enemy down and fight again while, back at headquarters, the commanders complained that the soldiers weren't fighting hard enough. Thanks to decent men like Syd Rowell, Tubby Allen and Pottsy, these grumblings did not reach the troops. Until Koitaki, the troops were kept safe from the commanders' venom.

On 8 and 9 September, Australian reinforcements reached the foothills of the Owen Stanley Range. The survivors of the 39th Battalion staggered back to Ilolo, located near the start of the Kokoda Track. These men, who had been fighting on the track since July, shrugged off their uniforms, which were now just rags, and bathed in the river.

Walking Wounded
Osmar White met two wounded men of the 39th Battalion out on the track. One had been shot in the foot, the other through the eye, the bullet entering just above the cheekbone and exiting behind the ear. He complained of headaches, but said the wound itself was not hurting. He walked, led by the man with the wounded foot. Together they had covered 113 miles, almost 200km, in 16 days.

The 39th were given time to recuperate and many during this period were sent to the Lightning Ridge Dysentery Hospital. Within weeks these soldiers were to be sent back over the track to Gona. Meanwhile, on day 48, 10 September, Potts was 'relieved' of duty by a temporary successor — Brigadier Selwyn Porter. General Headquarters was not happy with Potts's fighting withdrawal and wanted some forward action.

All the while MacArthur continued to downplay the threat of the Japanese force reaching Port Moresby. He considered that aggressive leadership was lacking in the Australian force and that the Australian soldiers were unable to match themselves against the Japanese in jungle combat.

Day 50, 12 September The Battle of Ioribaiwa
On day 47, the 25th Brigade of the AIF arrived in Port Moresby, equipped with jungle green uniforms. By day 49, 11 September, they were in

Soldiers of the 39th Battalion are relieved of their duty at the Kokoda front and make their way back to Ilolo.

position. Behind them, 25-pounder guns covered the Ioribaiwa ridge, waiting for the Japanese to come close enough. The line had been drawn.

Day 50 saw the Japanese prepare their troops for the final leg of their advance to Port Moresby. The Japanese army pressed on.

The Australians attacked the enemy and got a response, so the troops settled in and began probing the enemy's defence. Time was on their side, but sadly, their commanders were not.

The battle at Ioribaiwa lasted for three days and ended on day 54.

With the loss of Ioribaiwa, Brigadier Eather, commander of the 25th Brigade, sought a retreat to Imita Ridge. This last retreat rattled Port Moresby, and Eather received the message that further retreat was unacceptable. It was time to make a stand or die trying.

The Japanese Imperial Army could finally see the lights of Port Moresby and the glint of water beyond Port Moresby that is the Coral Sea. Three weeks after landing in New Guinea, the Nankai Shitai's 6000 combat troops had been reduced to 1500. More than one thousand were dead, sick or wounded and the rest were unaccounted for. General Horii was expecting an order to withdraw, but continued to behave as if his goal was Port Moresby.

There was very little food left to feed his troops. His supply line was 150 miles long. He dug in on the summit of Ioribaiwa and set about fortifying his position.

Day 63, 25 September The Japanese Retreat

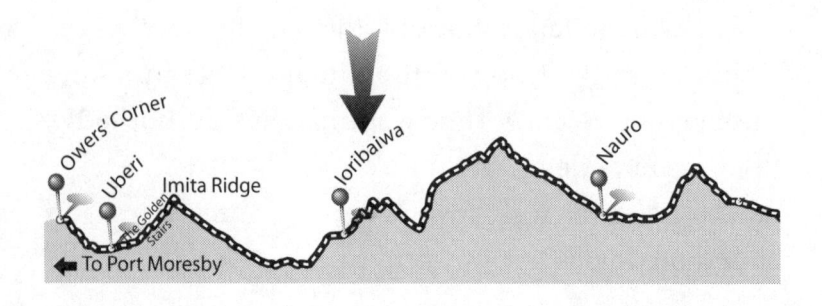

On day 58, Horii's deadline to invade Port Moresby came and went without further movement. On day 59, 21 September, the 2/2nd Battalion arrived in Port Moresby with 670 soldiers. On day 61, General Blamey arrived in Port Moresby to take charge and demanded instant action. Some people think he was there thanks to a ploy by MacArthur, who thought that Port Moresby would soon fall and that he wanted somebody there who could take the blame.

The Nankai Shitai troops had never retreated before. By 25 September, day 63, Horii ordered his officers to retreat. The Japanese advance up the track had worn itself out.

Shelling from Australian artillery cannon reached the Japanese positions later that morning. By the last week of September these troops were cut off by air and sea. On day 64, 26 September, the Australians pushed forward and found that the Japanese had started to retreat. The Japanese made a last ditch effort and fired a few rounds of their mountain gun upon the advancing Australian troops, but it was little use against the Australians' 25-pounder.

The 25th Brigade was ordered to attack Ioribaiwa on 28 September. More aircraft arrived, so that the entire length of the track could be patrolled to interfere with supply lines.

By this time the image of the 'Australian digger' had been transformed into a jungle-camouflaged,

Members of the 39th Battalion on 22 September 1942 on parade after fighting for weeks in the dense jungle on the Kokoda Track.

steel-helmeted, face-veiled fighter. The troops were now conquerors, not defenders.

Now the coast was clear for the senior commander to come and be seen. On day 70, 2 October, General MacArthur made a visit to Port Moresby. As usual, his subordinates played games with the truth. As George Johnston noted in his diary, two weeks later: 'Up here everybody is incensed at new censorship bans.' Apparently, MacArthur personally censorsed a report to convey that he went right up to the front line (which he certainly did not) and that this was *not* his first visit to New Guinea (which it was).

As the American troops had been told by their superiors, this was a war that was being fought to make the world safe for democracy.

Truth, it seems, was unimportant in such a war.

MacArthur claimed that the Australians were not fighting hard enough, and MacArthur had the ear of the Prime Minister, who was shaken by what MacArthur told him. Curtin then put pressure on Blamey, and Blamey put pressure on his generals to fight harder. This pressure passed on down the line. When generals refused to toe the line, Blamey sacked them, one after another.

On day 76, 8 October, MacArthur spent an hour with Blamey at the start of the track at Ower's Corner — about 17 km in from Sogeri — then returned to mess for lunch. He left for Brisbane the very next day. On day 77, 9 October, Arnold Potts was removed from command.

The lack of supplies was still a problem for the Australian troops. On day 79 the disorganisation of the supply threatened the viability of the Australian troops counter-offensive. Again, MacArthur could not, or would not, admit to the difficulties created by the terrain of the track. Of course, he could not fully understand what the soldiers were experiencing — he still had not been up the track.

There were no supplies in Nauro, the first Track depot, and none at Efogi on 9 October. Booby traps were also a problem for troops returning to abandoned camps. Even when supplies were dropped, the air-drops still lacked parachutes and a lot of supplies were lost.

Urging Them On

Later, in Australia, Allen spoke to MacArthur and explained the conditions the soldiers had endured on the Track, mentioning how much MacArthur's signals had distressed him. MacArthur said, 'But I've nothing but praise for you and your men. I was only urging you on.' Allen told him bluntly, 'Well, that's not the way to urge Australians.' But it was too late. The damage was done.

On day 79, 11 October, Brigadiers Lloyd and Eather attended a meeting in Tubby Allen's tent at Menari. Orders had come through from Blamey that day that the Australian troops were to capture Kokoda. A drop of supplies was arranged for Myola. Knowing that Blamey had never been up the track, Allen commented: 'This country is much tougher than any previous theatre and cannot be appreciated until seen.'

The Australian troops reached Templeton's Crossing around 15 October. A small detachment of Horii's troops remained dug in there. Meanwhile, Japanese reinforcements began to arrive at Templeton's Crossing and Eora Creek. After two days of fighting, the 2/2nd Battalion drove the Japanese out of the crossing. The two-day delay made MacArthur cantankerous and he aimed his anger at Blamey, by blaming the Australian officers. Blamey did nothing to counter MacArthur's attack, much to the distress of his officers.

By day 87, 19 October, about a third of the Japanese army were unfit for combat. The soldiers were supposedly given quinine tablets, but the Japanese were really not equipped to deal with malaria. Some doctors thought malaria was contagious among humans whilst others understood that the carrier was the swarms of mosquitoes that surrounded them day and night. Even so, doctors had no means to deal with the mosquitoes which contained the parasite.

On day 89, 21 October, Blamey insisted on the capture of Kokoda. Delay was getting dangerous as the Japanese reinforcements moved up to Eora Creek from Kokoda. On the 22nd, the 16th Brigade from the 6th Division reached Eora Creek. But the Japanese had a geographic advantage by digging into the high ridge above Eora Creek.

General Syd Rowell was dismissed and General Allen was left to take the full force of the attack from his superiors. He realised that Blamey and MacArthur thought ' ... the country is only undulating and that I could have swept around the flanks with a Brigade. Their ignorance of the situation was myopic. I was determined not to murder my men by letting them put me in a panic.'

When Allen took MacArthur and Blamey up to the jeep-head to be photographed on 7 October, there was an exchange that Allen later described to Gavin Long, the general editor of the official histories. Allen said that MacArthur argued that the

21st Brigade had not fought well. Allen answered that the brigade was as highly trained as any in the British and American armies, and that when the American troops had proved themselves to be as good, he would listen to MacArthur's remarks. Within a few days, Allen was dismissed.

On day 90, 22 October, Blamey withdrew Chester Wilmot's press accreditation. Wilmot had dared to write an appraisal of the Kokoda campaign and Blamey did not fare well in the analysis. Wilmot left the Pacific war to cover the war in Europe. Blamey phoned Potts on the same day and told Potts he would be moved to Darwin.

Blamey was looking for scapegoats and this was only the beginning.

On day 95, 27 October, Blamey replaced Major General Tubby Allen with Major General Vasey. That same day, the Australians charged the Japanese at Eora Creek. They charged again at dawn the next day.

By day 97, 29 October, the Australians had recaptured Eora and continued their march to Kokoda. More Australians died at Eora Creek than any other battle — except for Isurava — with 291 wounded or dead.

On day 98, 30 October, the sick and wounded at Myola were ordered to walk back to Port Moresby.

Major General Arthur (Tubby) Allen

Major General Arthur (Tubby) Allen was born in 1894, and after service in the cadets and the Australian Military Force, he was commissioned as a lieutenant in the AIF in 1915, ending the war in 1918 as a 24-year-old lieutenant colonel with a Distinguished Service Order (DSO), commanding the 13th Battalion in France.

He returned to civilian life, but stayed in the militia, and by 1938, he was a brigadier. In 1939, this experienced combat soldier went to the Middle East, commanding the 16th Brigade of the AIF. His brigade fought at Tobruk and in Greece, then in what is now Lebanon, where his troops fought the Vichy French.

He then returned to Australia, where he took charge of the Australian forces fighting the Japanese advance across New Guinea. Two commanders with far less experience of combat, Blamey and MacArthur, repeatedly attacked Allen for moving too slowly, and in the end, Blamey removed him from his command, shifting him to less important commands

Imagine you are there...

It wasn't easy carrying a wounded man on a stretcher. In training, they taught us to make a stretcher with two poles and a bit of rope wound around them with a blanket on top. I rode in one once, and it was quite comfortable, but that was along a road in Port Moresby. The real thing was a bit rougher, mainly because of the slopes.

There's no rope out in the jungle, but the carriers showed us how to cut a length of lawyer vine and whack it on a tree till the end split. Then you'd peel off a strip and use it. The strips were sort of flat, and with a blanket on top, they cut into you less than rope, and there was as much vine as you wanted. All the same, two poles weren't enough when you're on a slope, especially a slippery one.

There was this one old bloke called Dadima. He came from Daru and spoke English pretty well, once you realised that with his accent 'line' was really rain, and stuff like that. Anyhow, Dadima saw we didn't know much so he showed us how to lash a crosspiece at each end, which stopped the poles coming together and squashing the wounded bloke. These two extra bars gave more places to get a grip, and it stopped the wounded bloke sliding off the ends.

He was a villainous-looking old coot, and we were never sure about the yarns he told us. Someone asked him

one day how he knew so much about making stretchers.
Dadima replied that he was a cannibal and always carried
fresh meat home like that. He was always having a lend of
us. But while he liked a joke, he was always careful about
making the wounded safe and comfortable.

Every time you twist or tilt the stretcher, the wounded
bloke's likely to be hurt, or slide off. On dry, level
ground, two people can stand between the poles and
carry somebody their own weight, but in rough country,
you need four or more carriers, and you need a track
wide enough for three people to walk, side by side. If it's
slippery, you need spare people to steady the stretcher if
one of the carriers slips.

Each stretcher needs up to ten carriers. That's right
— ten. Going up a slope, the back has to be lifted high on
somebody's shoulders while the front is near the ground.
Going down, it's the other way around. To get over bad
country, you need two men between the poles, two more
on the outside of each of them, front and back, supporting
and steadying, and you need somebody to carry supplies
and food for the party. That gets you to seven carriers, but
in the worst bits, you need to pass the stretcher forward,
then move to the front, and pass again. That means three
teams of three, plus the gear carrier. So in bad country,
you needed ten to carry one wounded man safely.

It was pretty nasty for the wounded, because any jolt
was going to cause dreadful pain, so anybody who could
walk, even those who could only crawl, would prefer that
to being carried. Besides, they knew it was slowing down

the delivery of food and ammunition to the front line when they got carried. The blokes being carried out were the severe cases because the ones with less severe injuries or sickness were being kept near the front until they recovered so they could get back to the fighting again.

On 27 August, they sent 30 of the sickest and worst wounded of the 39th down the track, and I was one of them. I must have looked pretty crook, because I was out of it with malaria and I had a day of being carried. Mum's always said I was as tough as a Mallee bull. I reckon she was right. By the 28th but I started getting better, so I walked. By the 29th, 27 of us went back to the fight, all except a fellow with a bullet in his throat, another one missing a foot and one minus a forearm that had been blown away. The bloke with a bullet in his throat couldn't talk, but the other two called us all sorts of names because they couldn't come with us.

You do what you have to, but it gets harder as time goes on.

A wounded soldier is taken down the track to medical attention by native carriers affectionately known as the 'Fuzzy Wuzzy Angels'.

Chapter 10
101 Days — Australian Troops Enter Kokoda

Day 101, 2 November Re-entry Kokoda

Now the Australian troops were pushing forward, and on 2 November, the 101st day since the Australian troops set out to stop the Japanese advance over the track, the first Australian troops re-entered Kokoda village. The soldiers were jubilant. Doc Vernon was wheeled around by the villagers on a bicycle that had been abandoned by a Japanese soldier, outside the village.

Two days later, on 4 November, Bert Kienzle counted six American DC3s, all on the ground at the same time on Kokoda airstrip. If those aircraft had been available to land troops, artillery, ammunition and food at Kokoda in early July, the Japanese would never have passed that point. For the first time wounded could be flown back in safety to Port Moresby.

9 November Koitaki Speech

On day 108, 9 November, General Blamey turned up to address the survivors of the 2/14th and 2/16th battalions at Koitaki, a pleasant place in the Range above Port Moresby. He could get there by road, but even so, the troops must have felt pleased that the Australian Commander-in-Chief had made the effort to come and address them. Sure, the 39th had done well, but so had the two AIF battalions who had worn the enemy down until more troops could come and help wind the Japanese back.

A month earlier, Blamey had shouted at Brigadier Potts that the Owen Stanleys Campaign (as it was then called) was a complete failure. Even with the Japanese in full retreat, north of Kokoda, that was how he saw things in October.

According to the men who were at Koitaki, they understood all too clearly that the commander-in-chief stood before them and accused them of running like rabbits. Those who were there have always confirmed this version of events.

Later, Blamey explained that his speech had been misunderstood. He claimed he had said that while the Japanese were in their holes, they could not be shot, yet they could kill. That while the rabbits were in their burrows they could not be shot, but once they were on the run, the man with the gun could get them.

I believe Blamey's accusation of running like rabbits was unfounded. The handful of heroes on the track were all that stood between a powerful Japanese force and Port Moresby. Blamey insisted that the Australians outnumbered the Japanese, that they were better trained and equipped — things these battle-hardened survivors knew to be false.

Australian soldiers raise the Australian flag after forcing the Japanese Nankai Shitai out of Kokoda Village.

At all times the Australians had been outnumbered. They were trained in desert warfare (if they were in the AIF) or barely at all if in the militia. They knew nothing of jungle combat, yet they had held their own in a fighting withdrawal that wore the Japanese army down, delaying them and ensuring the Japanese attack was a failure. Then, as more troops came into the line, the Japanese were pushed back over the mountains. By the day of the Koitaki parade, Australian forces had reclaimed Kokoda and were chasing the Japanese down to the north coast.

During wartime, making disparaging remarks about an officer can get you into trouble. So the junior officers did their best to quieten the troops as grumblings against the general grew louder. The officers could do nothing when the troops were marched off and many of them deliberately did not give Blamey the 'eyes right' which is how soldiers salute commanders as they march past. They knew what Blamey had said.

And Blamey was not finished yet.

Once the soldiers left, he spoke to the officers. He told them he was unhappy with them. That they had failed to lead their troops. That they needed to pull up their socks.

This behaviour seems to back the agreed view about Blamey calling the AIF rabbits. The diggers were just waiting happily to be told what they knew, that they had done a brilliant job: there was no reason for them to invent a lie which had their commander turning against them.

Just 16 days later, Blamey's tune had completely changed. With MacArthur sending messages to his own generals to act 'regardless of losses' and 'at all costs', Blamey was scoring a few political points for Australia. The American troops around Buna were bogged down and getting nowhere and MacArthur suggested using the 41st American Division as reinforcements. Blamey turned down the offer of American troops, saying that he would prefer to use the 21st Brigade, even though it was under-strength 'as he knew they would fight'.

Perhaps he was playing politics with MacArthur. Or perhaps Blamey realised his error after visiting Australian troops in the hospital at Port Moresby. As he made his way past the wounded men, they ate lettuce leaves in front of him, twitched their noses and taunted him by whispering, 'Run, Rabbit, Run' behind his retreating back. Could that have made him start to think again?

During all this, Blamey said nothing at all about the 39th Battalion. He did not praise them. He did not thank them. He did not accuse them of running like rabbits. He seemed to be unaware of them. Perhaps he thought the 39th, as militia, could be expected to 'retreat', while the AIF had a duty to stand and be slaughtered. Perhaps he was unaware of the 550 heroic boys and men who had saved New Guinea — and his reputation — by holding the enemy up until the AIF battalions arrived.

The mob that wasn't

November, December and January saw the original Maroubra Force battalions — the 39th, the 2/14th and 2/16th — back in the thick of the fighting. New commanders worked them hard, and some say it was because they believed Blamey's lies — that these battalions had disgraced themselves and somehow needed to be punished.

In November 1942, the war shifted from the Kokoda Track to the northern coastal plain of Papua. The battle rules had changed again. Jungle warfare had turned to fighting in swamplands, grasslands and on beaches.

The Japanese saw the Papuan beachhead as an integral part of their campaign. They had built bunkers, pill boxes, heavily camouflaged machine-gun posts and tunnels.

The network of interconnecting tunnels was incredibly well hidden and mostly impervious to attack. The gunners lived in these tunnels for three months and only left them for night attacks and supplies.

Some estimated the Japanese numbers at 13,000, but they were later confirmed as 8000.

In mid-November, these bunkers were bombed from the air and hit by long range artillery. For the first

From the Battle

'Everywhere was mud...deep, oozing, slimy mud, grasping everything in its hungry maw. It was black mud, grimy black... The thunder of the big guns had become merely a nightmare echo — but the earth still trembled and the mud shivered like jelly.
Yes — like jelly... trembling. Men... trembling. The whole world...trembling.'
— Soldier, Q268941, *Khaki and Green*, published for The Australian Military Forces by Australian War Memorial Canberra, ACT, 1943.

time the Americans and Australians fought side by side.

At the beginning of December, the Allies needed fresh troops. Blamey chose the 39th Battalion resting in Port Moresby. The 39th returned to battle, along with 100 soldiers from the 53rd, to assist the Second Australian Imperial Force. The fresh troops joined the first concentrated attack on 6 December. Sadly, the soldiers of the much-maligned 53rd and 39th took the opportunity to display great heroics in response to Blamey's blast of cowardice. This almost suicidal courage ended in many needless deaths.

The campaign of Buna/Gona/Sanananda in late 1942 and early 1943 — the mopping-up drive to the north coast — was badly handled. It was a campaign that should have used air power far better, and in the end, a lot of Rowell's 'poor bastards' were killed or badly wounded to provide the glorious victory that the politicians and generals wanted.

The victory was that the Japanese forces were killed,

captured, or driven out of the area. It may have seemed less like a victory to the last men of the 39th.

The 39th had been there from the beginning of the Kokoda campaign. They might have been forgotten when Blamey lashed out at the AIF men at Koitaki, but by January 1943, there were very few of them left to be sent back to Port Moresby. When the survivors of the original 550 battalion members of the 39th left Sanananda, there were just 7 officers and 25 'other ranks' able to travel. To do so, they had first to get to the airfield at Dobodura. They were worn out, but when Colonel Honner asked for transport for his men, it was refused.

Here is how Honner told the story: 'The edict from Brigade was that transport would be provided to pick up all stragglers, but the battalion would march to Dobodura. I said, "The 39th Battalion won't have any stragglers, you won't need to pick any of them up."'

In fact, the 39th marched to Dobodura, mostly in columns with men supporting the least fit soldiers. Trucks rushed past them with cheering troops, many of whom were stragglers who hadn't seen much fighting.

When the 39th reached Dobodura they reformed into a parade ground formation of one single line. They marched across the airfield and drew a crowd as people came outside to see the unusual sight.

One of the spectators said, 'What mob's this?'

'We ignored them,' said Honner, 'looking straight ahead and marching at attention. But my 2/IC marching at the end of the line barked, "This is not a mob, this is the 39th!"'

Indeed they were!

Why is it important?

At first, the troops of Maroubra Force thought they were fighting to save an airstrip, to win a battle that would maybe help win a war. By the time other troops came to support them, the Australians believed that they were fighting to defeat a Japanese attempt to invade Australia.

We know now that the Japanese high command had ruled out trying to invade Australia. It was just too big an area, and it would have taken too many soldiers to try and control an area that would be handy, but which was not essential. They had the minerals, the oil, the rubber and the rice they wanted from the Asian countries they controlled, so they could afford to wait.

The Japanese plan was to surround Australia, to make it impossible for the US to use it as a base, so that they could fight the US to a standstill. Then, when the Japanese had Australia surrounded and peace was made, they could have cut a deal which saw Australia as a colony of Japan — a place that would supply the raw materials Japan needed.

To do this the Japanese had to capture Port Moresby. Thanks to US naval forces and the Australian army, they never did manage to do that. Mind you, MacArthur's followers had a different slant on the whole affair.

MacArthur's former senior intelligence officer, Major General Charles A. Willoughby, explained in a 1956 book that the Japanese had to be stopped from crossing a 14,000-foot range! And that General MacArthur and his staff moved personally to Port Moresby, where they joined a handful of Australians who had come to prospect for gold and stayed to fight.

When General MacArthur arrived in Port Moresby on 6 November, the fighting was almost over, and it was certainly nowhere near the jeep head which was as close as he ever got. The Australians had entered Kokoda four days before, and the first American troops had yet to take the field in New Guinea. There were, however, significant numbers of US Air Force personnel there doing sterling service.

Forget MacArthur — the American airmen made it possible for the Australians to win.

The militia battalions, the AIF battalions and the Papuan Infantry Battalion all fought to keep out a fierce and dangerous enemy.

They were betrayed all along the way by most of their senior generals. In spite of Blamey and

MacArthur, these brave soldiers defeated the Japanese.

The lessons

In my youth, my generation scoffed at the Anzac tradition. We saw Anzac day as a chance for a bunch of old soldiers to get drunk and play two-up, but time has brought understanding and empathy for these men. We recognise and celebrate the sacrifices and bravery of our soldiers — ordinary men and women — who took a stand and defended our right to freedom.

If you ever visit Gallipoli and cross the water to Canakkale after the dawn service, you may see the Turks celebrating their victory, and no Australian or New Zealander would begrudge them their celebration. Some Anzac celebrations in Australia even have Turkish guests.

If you looked for a grand Australian World War II victory to remember, there are two possibilities. Milne Bay was the first time that the Japanese lost, and they were defeated by a much larger force. For true heroism, you can't go past the victory that was won against a far more powerful, better-trained and better-equipped enemy by Maroubra Force on days 33 to 36 of the 101 days of the Kokoda Track campaign. It's a celebration of the fighting withdrawal employed by those brave soldiers.

Of conceding ground to live to fight another day.

Of losing a battle to win the war.

Timeline

1901: Australia becomes an independent nation as Australian troops fight for Britain in the Boer War in South Africa

1914: World War I starts in Europe

1915: Anzac forces land in Gallipoli in a futile attack

1916-1918: Australian troops are bogged down in trench warfare in France

1918: end of World War I

1931: Japanese army invades Manchuria in China

1935: Italy invades Abyssinia (Ethiopia) to make it a colony

1936, April: civil war in Spain starts. German forces take part and practise new tactics

1937-1938: Japanese army massacres more than 300,000 Chinese in Nanking

1938, March: German army invades Austria

1938, October: German army invades Sudetenland, part of Czechoslovakia

1939, March: German army invades the rest of Czechoslovakia

1939, April: Spanish civil war ends

1939, September: Germany invades Poland, World War II begins

1940: Japan signs a mutual cooperation pact with Germany and Italy

1941, 7 October: John Curtin becomes Prime Minister of Australia

1941, 7 December: Japan bombs Pearl Harbor, attacks Malaya

1942: Japanese army occupies much of south-east Asia

1942, 23 January: The Japanese capture Rabaul, capital of New Britain

1942, 15 February: Singapore surrenders to Japan

1942, 19 February: Japanese air raids on Darwin

1942, March: Japanese troops land at Lae on the island of New Guinea

1942, 8 March: Japanese forces land at Lae and Salamaua on the north coast of New Guinea

1942, 9 March: 20,000 Australian troops arrived at Adelaide and Perth.

1942, May: the Battle of the Coral Sea turns back a Japanese invasion of Port Moresby from the sea

1942, 30 & 31 May: Japanese midget submarines attack in Sydney Harbour

1942, 21 July: Japanese troops land at Buna, at the northern end of the Kokoda Track

1942, 29 July: the 39th are driven out of Kokoda

1942, 26 August: Japanese attack Isurava and Japanese Marines land at Milne Bay. The 39th Battalion holds the Japanese off, slowing them down until AIF troops arrive.

1942, 30 August: Fall of Isurava to the Japanese force.

1942, 6 September: Cyril Clowes' troops defeat the Japanese at Milne Bay

1942, 2 October: Australian troops work their way back over the track, wearing the Japanese down, then they roll forward again

1942, 29 October: Australians win the battle of Eora Creek

1942, 2 November: Australian troops re-enter Kokoda

1942, 9 November: Blamey's infamous 'running like rabbits' speech at Koitaki Cricket Ground

1942, 19 November: The Americans arrive and join the Australian troops against the Japanese

1942, 28 November: 21st Brigade joins the troops at Gona

1942, 9 December: Australians drive Japanese out of Gona

1943, January: the last Japanese resistance on the northern coast of New Guinea is wiped out

1945: end of World War II

Glossary

AIF: the Australian Imperial Force was made up of volunteers and could be directed to serve anywhere. The Second AIF served in World War II. Battalions of the AIF had a "2/" in front of their number.

Allied Powers: In the early days of the war against Japan, they were referred to as ABDA— American, British, Dutch and Australian.

Battalion: comprised of up to 1000 men, soldiers and support crew. However the number was often 550 or fewer. Made up of five companies (A, B, C, D and HQ), and commanded by a lieutenant colonel.

Bren gun: a light machine gun that fired standard 0.303 cartridges from a magazine holding 30 rounds.

Brigade: three battalions, commanded by a brigadier.

Carrier: a man from any of the islands, but usually from Papua, New Guinea or New Britain, who worked on contract to carry ammunition, food, supplies or wounded soldiers.

Company: three platoons, totalling about 110 soldiers.

Division: Typically three brigades, commanded by a major general.

Dixie: a large cooking pot, or a set of two nesting tins that can be used to cook food.

DSO: Distinguished Service Order, a medal usually awarded to a senior officer for success in battle.

General: A senior-commander. A brigadier is the same as an American one-star general, and the ranks above are major general and lieutenant general.

Machine gun: a gun that fires bullets one after another, automatically.

Malaria: a disease caused by parasites in the blood, which is spread by mosquitoes. It causes a fever, and can be fatal.

Mentioned in Dispatches: MID. A dispatch is a senior commander's report to his superiors. Soldiers who performed noteworthy actions that were written about in the dispatch, were said to have been 'mentioned in dispatches'. MID is an award, though the soldier is not given a medal.

MC: Military Cross, a medal awarded to officers for bravery.

MM: Military Medal, a medal awarded to Privates and NCOs for bravery.

Militia: a section of the army that is similar to the army reserve. They could only serve in Australian territory.

Mortar: light-weight portable artillery. When a shell is loaded into the mortar, a pin at the bottom sets off an explosive charge, which fires the shell at short range.

Mountain gun: a gun that fired explosive shells. It was designed to be taken apart into pieces that could be carried separately.

NCO: a non-commissioned officer such as a lance corporal, corporal, sergeant, or warrant officers.

New Guinea Infantry Battalions (NGIB): comprised of soldiers from New Guinea. There were four NGIBs.

Pearl Harbor: a US naval base on the Hawaiian island of Oahu.

PIB: the Papuan Infantry Battalion was an army force of Papuan soldiers. Together with four New Guinea Infantry Battalions, they formed the Pacific Islands Regiment.

Platoon: three sections, totalling about 35 soldiers.

Rifle: The Lee-Enfield .303 was standard World War II issue. It weighed just over 4 kilograms, used a bolt-action to reload, and carried a magazine with 10 rounds.

Section: a group of about eleven soldiers who fight as a unit.

Sigs: signalmen, or 'Sigs' worked along the track, operating and stringing telephone wires that were used to communicate to and from headquarters.

Singapore: where the main British base in Southeast Asia was located.

Sniper: a sharpshooter who operates from a hidden position.

Sulfa drugs: a treatment for infected wounds.

Vichy French: the French who allied themselves with the Germans, and fought on their side.

Victoria Cross: the highest award for valour in the face of the enemy. Rarely awarded, and often given posthumously.

War correspondent: a journalist who travels with the forces, and reports back on what has happened.

Acknowledgments

This book could not have been written if the Australians in Maroubra Force had not overcome amazing odds. This is their story.

I could not have gathered so much detail if it had not been for the dedicated people at the Australian War Memorial who have preserved the stories.

I became aware of many of the facts while reading the standard histories, and they sent me fossicking in many directions. I owe a special debt of gratitude to the war correspondents who saw through the MacArthur and Blamey publicity machines, and got the true story out.

I had special help from my uncle Bill Macinnis and my cousin Iain Macinnis. They are both retired career members of the armed forces, and were able to point me in unexpected directions. Iain helped me to access Jim Cowey's service record, and to understand it.

I actually wrote this book twice. The first time was a disaster, because I zeroed in on the injustice done at Koitaki, and my story line concentrated on that, instead of the real story, the ingenious efforts of a small Australian force to outfight a much larger force.

My thanks to the nice people at Black Dog who persuaded me to tell the story a different way — to tell a different story, in fact!

black dog thanks Dr Karl James from the Australian War Memorial for fact checking and for reading the manuscript.

References

Baker, Clive, *Walking the Kokoda trail: do-it-yourself trekking guide*. Loftus, NSW, Australian Military History Publications, 1994.

Braga, Stuart, *Kokoda commander : a life of Major-General "Tubby" Allen*. South Melbourne, Oxford University Press, 2004.

Browne, Margaret (illustrated by Hans Selhofer), *The Kokoda campaign*. Lane Cove, Hodder and Stoughton, 1985.

Brune, Peter, *A Bastard of a Place*. Sydney, Allen and Unwin, 2003.

Brune, Peter, *The Spell Broken*. Sydney, Allen and Unwin, 1997.

Brune, Peter, *Those Ragged Bloody Heroes*. Sydney, Allen and Unwin, 1991.

Brune, Peter, *We Band of Brothers*. Sydney, Allen and Unwin, 2000.

Clark, Sylvia (illustrated by Elizabeth Pickhaver-Burness), *The Kokoda Track*. Kenthurst, NSW, Kangaroo Press, 1997.

FitzSimons, Peter, *Kokoda*. Sydney, Hodder Headline, 2004.

Ham, Paul, *Kokoda*. Sydney, HarperCollins, 2004.

Johnston, George, *War Diary 1942*. Sydney, William Collins, 1984.

Lindsay, Patrick, *The Spirit of Kokoda*. Melbourne, Hardie Grant Books, 2002.

McAulay, Lex, *Blood and iron: the battle for Kokoda 1942*. Sydney, Hutchinson, 1991.

McCarthy, Dudley, *South-West Pacific Area — First Year*. Canberra, Australian War Memorial, 1959.

McDonald, Neil, *Chester Wilmot Reports*. Sydney, ABC Books, 2004.

Paull, Raymond, *Retreat from Kokoda: the Australian campaign in New Guinea 1942*. Melbourne, Heinemann, 1958.

Phillips, WHJ, *The Miracle of Kokoda*. Coffs Harbour, Phillips Productions, 2000.

White, Osmar, *Green Armour*. Sydney, Angus and Robertson, 1945.

Photos/Illustration Credits

Front Cover photo: 25-Pounder guns being pulled through dense jungle in the vicinity of Uberi on the Kokoda Track. AWM Image Number 026855.

Back Cover photo: Australian and American soldiers gaze at Salamaua. AWM Image Number 015394.

Page vi and vii: Three-dimensional map of Kokoda Track by Guy Holt Design

Page vi and vii: Diagram of Kokoda Track by Guy Holt Design.

Page 24: 26 March 1942. General MacArthur with General Sir Thomas Blamey and the Prime Minister, Mr Curtain. AWM ID 042766.

Page 27: Illustration courtesy of www.cyber-heritage.co.uk

Page 29: Guy Holt Design.

Page 35: Private P. Shimmin of the 2/33rd AIF starts on his daily ration of bully beef. AWM ID Number 027062.

Page 53: Sappers of the 2/14th Australian Field Company Royal Australian Engineers begin building a road between Port Moresby and Kokoda. AWM ID Number 026310.

Page 77: Illustration courtesy of www.cyber-heritage.co.uk

Page 92: Imita Ridge, Papua. Two native carriers and a member of 2/4th Field Ambulance slowly climb the so-called 'Golden Stairs' towards Ioribaiwa in October 1942. AWM ID Number P02423.009.

Page 99: Osmar White, Melbourne Herald correspondent, and Chester Wilmot of the Australian Broadcasting Commission at their camp on the Kokoda front. (Negative by Parer.) AWM ID 01347.

Page 131: Private Bruce Steel Kingsbury VC, 2/14th Infantry Battalion was awarded the Victoria Cross posthumously for action in the Isurava. AWM ID 100112.

Page 143: Some members of D Company, 39th Battalion, returning to their base camp after at battle at Isurava. AWM ID Number 013288.

Page 146: Members of the 39th Battalion, AMF, parade after

weeks of fighting in dense jungle during the Kokoda Campaign. AWM ID Number 013289.

Page 155: Indigenous (native) New Guinea stretcher bearers (popularly known as fuzzy wuzzy angels) carry a wounded soldier down a muddy track through the jungle. AWM ID P02110.001.

Page 158: November 1942, Kokoda, the Australian flag is hoisted. AWM Image Number 013603.

Index

21st Brigade, 74, 83, 85, 150, 160, 168
30th Brigade, 34, 37, 39, 71
39th Battalion 3, 4, 7, 8, 9, 25, 28, 34, 48, 70, 71, 73, 74, 75, 81, 83, 115, 121, 122, 124, 125, 128, 141, 142, 155, 160, 161, 163, 164, 168, 173
— fighting withdrawal, 5, 79, 83, 105, 108, 112, 113, 137, 139, 157
— origins, 33, 37, 38, 39, 126
— Maroubra, 49, 56, 57
— Port Moresby, 32, 33
49th Battalion, 32, 37
53rd Battalion, 37–8, 49, 113, 115, 126

Allen, Major General, 85, 141, 148–151, 172
Allied Headquarters, 43
Allied Powers, 17, 169
Allies, 15, 41, 59, 98, 100, 135, 137, 162
Anzac Day, 7
Anzacs, 128

Battle of the Coral Sea, 4, 39, 42, 168
Battle of Midway, 4, 17, 42
Bidstrup, Captain Max, 67–8, 72–3
Blamey, General Sir Thomas,
— 39th Battalion, 162–3
— and Allen, 151
— and Wilmot, 96, 97
— before World War II, 23–25
— Koitaki Speech, 156–7, 159–160, 163, 168

Bren gun, 68, 74, 76–7, 131, 169
Brigade Hill, 140–1
British Empire, 13–4, 19
Buna, 4, 47, 49, 160, 162, 168
Butcher's Hill, 140

camouflage, 96–7, 103, 122, 125, 145, 161
chockos, 4, 108, 121
Churchill, Prime Minister Sir Winston, 18–20
code(s) (decoded messages), 23, 41, 44, 59, 98, 112, 115, 136
Commander-in-Chief of the Australian Military Forces, 22
Cowey, Sergeant Major Jim, 75, 79–82, 106
Curtin, Prime Minister John, 18–21, 26, 147, 167

Darwin, 21, 150, 167
dengue fever, 34
Deniki, 61, 62, 66, 69–71, 73, 75, 80, 82–3
Dobodura, 44, 136, 163
dysentery, 34, 140, 142

Eather, Brigadier, 144, 148
Efogi, 130, 137, 139–140, 147
Eora Creek, 130, 132, 148–150, 168

Gallipoli, 7, 24, 71, 85–6, 128, 133, 166–7
gap, 91, 93, 138

General Headquarters (GHQ), 30, 116, 138
Gona, 4, 49, 55, 84, 142, 162, 168
Gorari, 60

Harukichi, Lieutenant General Hyakutake, 42
Herring, Lieutenant General Edmund, 135
Honner, Lieutenant Colonel Ralph, 34, 114–5, 123, 124, 128, 134, 139, 163–4

Imperial Army, 42, 101, 144
Ioribaiwa, 5, 142–145
Isurava, 3, 33, 61, 89, 112, 113, 117, 123, 124, 126, 128–9, 131, 150, 168

Japanese navy, 16, 42
Johnston, George, 93, 96, 98, 100, 104, 146, 172

Kienzle, Bert, 50–2, 55, 117, 135, 156
Kingsbury, Private Bruce Steel, 129, 131
Koitaki, 50, 141, 156–7, 159, 163, 168, 171
Kokoda, airstrip, 43–4, 50, 57–59, 62, 66–7, 69, 72–3, 75, 78, 80, 104–5, 113, 134, 156, 164
Kokoda, village, 5, 55, 58–9, 156

lawyer vine, 94–5, 152
League of Nations, 15
Lloyd, Brigadier, 148

MacArthur, General Douglas, 21–23, 40, 41, 44, 90, 93–4, 100, 112, 116, 118, 136, 138–9, 142, 145–151, 160, 165–6, 171
malaria, 34, 71, 102, 149, 154, 169
Maroubra Force, 48–9, 56, 84, 137, 161, 164, 166, 171
Menzies, Prime Minister Robert, 13, 17, 20
Merritt, Lieutenant William, 38
Metson, Corporal John Arthur, 13
Middle East, 5, 11, 14, 25, 97, 104, 151
Military Cross (MC), 71, 81, 84–5
Mills grenade, 27
Mission Ridge, 140
Morris, Major General, 39, 43, 47–8, 52, 57, 67, 68, 105
Myola, 83, 116–7, 119, 130, 140, 148, 150

Nankai Division, 4, 42, 144–5
Nimitz, US Admiral, 41–2
Oivi, 61, 62, 66, 72
Owen Stanley Range, 3, 4, 10, 36, 39, 44, 58, 59, 68, 107, 130, 137–8, 141
Owen, Lieutenant Colonel W.T., 57, 62, 66–7, 69, 72
Ower's Corner, 147
Papuan Infantry Battalion (PIB), 47, 49, 55–57, 61, 71, 137, 165, 170
Parer, Damien, 97–98
Pearl Harbor, 16–17, 167, 170
Philippines, 14, 21, 22, 44
Port Moresby, 3–10, 25, 32–34, 36–7, 39–47, 50, 51, 55, 57, 59, 66–7, 69–72, 74, 76, 78, 83–85, 90, 96, 101, 105, 107, 113, 116–7, 121–123, 130, 136–7, 142, 143–146, 150, 152, 156–7, 160, 162–3, 165, 168
Porter, Brigadier Selwyn, 37–8, 142

Potts, Brigadier Arnold, 75, 83–85, 116, 126–7, 140–142, 147, 150, 157

Rabaul, 15, 17, 36, 39, 41, 43–4, 57, 71, 130, 136, 167
Roosevelt, President Franklin D., 16, 19, 21
Rowell, Lieutenant General Sydney, 39–40, 43–44, 100, 118, 129–130, 135, 138–9, 141, 149, 162
Royal Australian Air Force (RAAF), 14
Russell, William, 98

Sanopa, Lance Corporal, 61, 62, 75
Second Australian Imperial Force (2/AIF), 4
Seven-mile Strip, 9, 74, 117
Simonson, Lieutenant, 82–3, 107, 125
Singapore, 6, 14, 16, 17, 167, 170
sniper, 8–9, 122, 131, 170
Sogeri, 51–2, 90, 147
Sydney, 21, 33, 35, 168
Symington, Captain, 72, 75, 78–9
Syria, 15, 19, 84, 85, 89, 121

Templeton, Lieutenant Sam, 38, 48, 60–1, 70, 148
Thompson gun, 76, 79
Tomitaro, Major General Horii, 42, 114, 115, 117, 123, 130, 135, 144–5, 148
tropical ulcers, 34–5, 87

Vasey, Major General George, 150
Vernon, Captain Geoffrey, 69–71, 135, 156
Vichy French, 15, 85, 151, 170
Victoria Cross (VC), 129, 131

Wairopi, 58, 60
war baby, 7
White, Osmar, 96–99, 106–7, 129, 142, 172
Wilmot, Chester, 40, 94, 96–98, 103, 117, 150, 172

Yokoyama Advance Force Unit, 4

The Drum: Inside information: reliable, confidential, or profitable: to give someone the drum

Scarecrow Army: the Anzacs at Gallipoli
by Leon Davidson

"the story of the retreat alone is a fascinating account of miliary tactics…A terrific book…" — *The West Australian*

Winner, 2006 New Zealand Post Book Awards, winner 2006 CBCA Eve Pownall Award, shortlisted LIANZA children's book awards

Red Haze: Australians and New Zealanders in Vietnam
by Leon Davidson

"Well focused, undistracted account of the origins and nature of the war…Davidson puts the reader at one with the soldiers…a compelling book written with a deft touch." — *Viewpoint*

Joan of Arc: the Story of Jehanne Darc
by Lili Wilkinson

Alexander the Great: Reckless Conqueror
by Carole Wilkinson

Fire in the Belly: the Inside Story of the Modern Olympics
by Carole Wilkinson

Fly a Rebel Flag: the Battle at Eureka
by Robyn Annear, shortlisted, 2004 NSW Premier's Young People's History Prize

Black Snake: the Daring of Ned Kelly
by Carole Wilkinson
Honour book, CBCA

DATE DUE